THE ULTIMATE GUIDE TO HANDGUN HUNTING

Tips and Tactics for Hunting Small and Big Game

CLAIR REES

The Lyons Press
Guilford, Connecticut
An imprint of The Globe Pequot Press

DEDICATION

Ten thousand thanks to Lynn Thompson, Larry Kelly, J. D. Jones, Ted Nugent, Dwight Van Brunt, Tim Janzen, Thompson/Center, SSK Industries and Mag-na-port International for their invaluable contributions to this book. Thanks also to Dave Scovill, editor of Successful Hunter, *who graciously allowed me to excerpt sections of articles I originally authored for his magazine.*

The Lyons Press is an imprint of The Globe Pequot Press.

Printed in the United States of America

10 9 8 7 6 5 4 3 2 1

ISBN 1-58574-820-X

Library of Congress Cataloging-in-Publication Data is available on file.

CONTENTS

INTRODUCTION: WHY HUNT WITH A HANDGUN

Why hunt with a handgun? There's a simple answer. Hunting with any handgun offers considerably greater reward and satisfaction than you'll experience when carrying a rifle afield. Handguns make a fun, challenging sport even more fun and challenging. Pistol and revolver hunting requires considerably more skill than hunting with a long-range rifle. Handguns test your patience and stalking abilities. When you hunt with these short-barreled firearms, success is simply sweeter.

Handgun hunters and bowhunters have a lot in common. Increasing the level of difficulty lowers the chance of scoring, but boosts hunting enjoyment. Taking game with a pistol or revolver provides a real sense of accomplishment. When you do something out of the ordinary, you savor each success.

With the right firearm and a good scope, an experienced rifleman can cleanly kill game at three hundred yards or more. At the other end of the scale, bowhunters typically limit their shots to twenty or thirty yards; and forty yards is extreme range even for experienced archers. To kill with a bow, you have to be close. People choose these short-range hunting tools precisely because they welcome the challenge.

Handguns fall somewhere between bows and rifles in terms of effective range. Those who use revolvers equipped with iron (not telescopic) sights have only a small edge over bowhunters. For me, sure-kill range for an open-sighted sixgun is just shy of fifty yards. Some handgunners you'll meet later in this book have the skill to confidently connect at nearly twice that distance. Long-barreled pistols chambered for high-intensity rifle rounds can double that range again, but only in the hands of experienced shooters using long-eye-relief magnifying sights.

It takes considerable practice to shoot a handgun well. Before you carry any kind of handgun afield, you should be able to keep all your shots on a eight-inch paper plate at game-getting range. That's a bare minimum requirement. If you can't do this consistently at fifty yards, your marksmanship needs more work. I'm talking about shooting from your two hind legs—not from a sandbagged rest. Once you've attained this expertise, do your best to avoid shooting at game offhand. Whenever possible, drop to the kneeling or sitting position, or use a handy tree to steady your handgun. Don't let the tree come in direct con-

tact with the gun, though. Use your (gloved) hand as a buffer or the shot could go wild. Better yet, carry one of the light, compact, highly portable bipods now available and use it every chance you get.

An ever-increasing number of sportsmen are turning to handguns—not just for hunting deer, but for all types of game.

Handgun hunters using open sights have only a small edge over bowhunters. Sure-kill range for an iron-sighted sixgun is less than fifty yards.

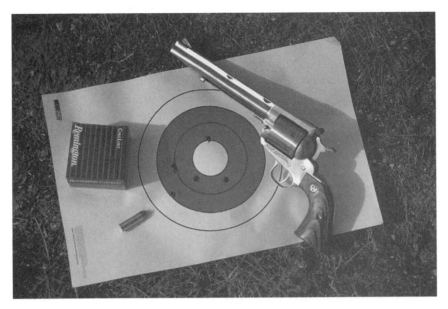

Before hunting with a handgun, be sure you can place all your shots within an eight-inch circle for the distance at which you'll be shooting.

HANDGUNS ADD CHALLENGE

Because handgun marksmanship can be difficult to master, pistol-packing nimrods face a pair of added challenges over their rifle-toting friends. Stalking and shooting skills must be honed to a much finer edge when handguns replace rifles in the hunting field. The first problem is getting within effective shooting range, which varies with the type of handgun used and the marksmanship skills of the user. This means getting as close as possible—if you're carrying an iron-sighted revolver, think "bowhunting range."

You must pass up those long shots you'd reasonably take with a rifle. Experienced bowhunters regularly manage to get within twenty or thirty yards of their quarry, so—with practice and patience—there's no reason you can't do the same. If you have difficulty moving stealthily enough to work your way into handgunning range, do what I did the first time I hunted deer with a handgun. Find yourself a likely ambush spot with some brush to break up your outline, then assume a comfortable sitting position and stay put. If you're hunting whitetail during the rut, rattling or calling can bring deer on the run. When the timing is right, rattling is probably the most effective way to lure a whitetail buck into easy handgun range.

Hunting handgunners score less often—a fact antihunters will applaud—but today's true sportsmen are more concerned with the quality of the hunting experience than with bringing home fresh venison.

Not all handguns are limited to fifty or seventy-five yards. Some single-shot pistols chambered for high-intensity rifle rounds shoot flat enough (and accurately enough) to hit small targets at 150 or 200 yards. A scope-equipped Thompson/Center G2 Conten-

Deer taken with a handgun provide a higher degree of satisfaction than those taken with a rifle because the challenge is greater.

der chambered for the .223 Remington cartridge, for example, is a fine choice for shooting prairie dogs, ground squirrels, and other small rodents at ranges normally reserved for riflemen. The similar but stronger Thompson/Center Encore chambered for cartridges like the 7mm-03, .308, or .30–06 is capable of taking deer and other large game at very respectable distances.

Of course, long-range marksmanship with a handgun requires even greater skill than the average pistoleer possesses. But that's all part of the game. The more practiced you become, the more successfully you'll hunt.

HUNTING SIGHTS

Handgunning at extended ranges—anything much over fifty yards—is greatly simplified by the addition of a magnifying scope sight designed specifically for handguns. The factory iron sights

Long-eye-relief pistol scopes increase precision for shooting at longer ranges.

supplied on most revolvers and auto pistols are too coarse for satisfactory shooting at extended range. At one hundred yards, a handgun's iron sights will entirely hide a deer's lower body.

The scope's crosshair reticle allows you to place your bullets exactly where you want them to go. In addition, the optics help clarify distant targets and can be particularly helpful in low light. A good scope adds several minutes to each end of a hunter's day by providing improved vision at dawn and dusk.

Unlike rifle scopes, which must be held within three or four inches of the shooter's eye, handgun scopes have considerably greater eye relief. This allows a clear view of the reticle and target with the handgun held at arm's length. This extended eye-to-lens distance makes for a considerably smaller sight picture. The shooter's eye must also be stationed almost directly behind the lens to see through the scope.

Because it's so difficult to hold a scoped handgun steady, most handgun scopes are of low power. A scope that doubles the size of the target image (2X) is a good choice for most hunting purposes, and few revolver fans opt for more than 4X magnification. There are 3–9X and even 3–12X variable handgun scopes on the market, but these are for long-range varmint hunting or target use. It takes a very solid rest with the gun supported by sandbags or some other external support to hold a handgun steady enough to make practical use of a 6X or 7X scope.

With electronic red-dot sights, the shooter simply superimposes the dot directly over the target as he squeezes the trigger. Because the sight provides no magnification, it can be used with both eyes open. This makes electronic sights extremely fast to use, and they provide excellent mid-range accuracy.

Adding any kind of scope or electronic sight to a handgun makes the gun twice as bulky and three times harder to carry. A shoulder holster designed specifically for scoped handguns is the only practical way to tote such a combination, and only a custom-made rig will accommodate a pistol or revolver with a Holosight or red-dot sight. Otherwise, you simply have to carry the gun in your hand.

HANDGUNS FOR HUNTING DEER

Hunting deer-sized game with handguns was once considered a novelty, and it wasn't even legal in many areas. Today, most states accept handgun hunters as legitimate sportsmen. The handgun is in widespread use during deer season, although nearly all game laws require firearms shooting .357 magnum, .44 magnum, or more potent cartridges for this purpose. (Rabbits, foxes, coyotes, and other small game are also hunted with handguns, and no such caliber limitations apply.)

Deer have fallen to less powerful cartridges than the .357 magnum, but most hunters regard even this round as marginal for deer-sized game. The .41 and .44 magnums kick a bit harder, but they're much better choices for the deer woods. Far more potent revolver rounds like the .454 Casull,

A well-designed shoulder holster offers one practical way to carry a scoped handgun afield.

Many hunters simply carry their handgun in their hands.

.480 Ruger, and the king-of-the-hill .500 Smith & Wesson are suited for even larger game.

These represent the upper practical power limit for revolver rounds, but single-shot handguns designed expressly for hunting offer rifle-like performance at effective ranges.

HUNTING LARGE AND SMALL GAME

Handguns can be used to take large game like moose, elk, or even Alaskan grizzlies. To down such oversized beasts, handgunners must get very close and place their bullets with cool precision. Remember, the .44 magnum—at one time the "world's most powerful handgun cartridge"—hits with less than half the punch generated by a .30–30 rifle round at one hundred yards. Today, the .30–30 is regarded as a pretty weak sister, although this round has been a popular deer load for nearly a century and has accounted for millions of deer.

Handguns have taken many of Alaska's giant grizzlies. Larry Kelly shot this bear with his Stalker version of Ruger's single-action .44 magnum.

No game is too large for a well-placed shot from a magnum handgun—including African elephant. Photo courtesy of Larry Kelly.

Many of the giant Alaskan grizzlies killed with handguns have been helped along by rifle-toting guides. Handguns have taken the largest, most dangerous game on earth, but prudence (and in most cases, hunting regulations) dictates having a licensed guide or professional hunter with a bigbore rifle handy in case backup is required.

At the other end of the scale, rabbits, squirrels, and other small game can be taken with a rimfire pistol or revolver. Handguns chambered for .22 Long Rifle, .22 Magnum, or .17 Hornady Magnum Rimfire rounds are capable of doing an excellent job out to fifty yards or so. While .22 and .17 Rimfire Magnum ammo costs more, .22 Long Rifle pistols and revolvers are inexpensive to own and operate. These guns are considerably quieter than centerfires, and are much more pleasant to shoot.

Auto pistols are okay for small game, but most don't digest ammo potent enough for deer and larger animals. Autoloaders chambered for the .38 Super, .357 SIG, or 9mm Parabellum shoot flat enough for 75- to 100-yard kills on rabbits, foxes, and the like, but lack the necessary *oomph* for bigger beasts. Exceptions to this rule include the 10mm and potent .50 Action Express (AE) loads.

Hunting revolvers can be of either the double-action or western-styled single-action variety. Hunters almost invariably cock the hammer before they shoot, so the single-action thumb-buster is at no real disadvantage here. But if you were facing a bad-tempered bruin at close quarters, the ability to fire fast follow-up shots with a double-action would be highly comforting.

SHOOTING SKILLS

Hunting handgunners must practice until they thoroughly master their firearms. A poor marksman is no real sportsman. Until you can place all your shots into that eight- or nine-inch paper

Auto pistols chambered for .22 Long Rifle rimfires are good for hunting rabbits and other small game.

plate at fifty yards or so while shooting from a hunting position you're not ready to hunt deer-sized game with a handgun.

Hunting smaller game demands even greater accuracy, but a bad shot is more likely to cleanly miss a rabbit-sized mark. With deer-sized game, a poorly placed round is apt to injure the animal and cause a painful, lingering death. If you're not sure you can hit a vital spot with your first shot, hold your fire.

Handguns are becoming increasingly popular among hunters, but game laws vary from state to state. Be sure to confirm the legality of handgun hunting in your area, and that your handgun meets game law requirements, before going afield. Because handgun bullets can travel several hundred yards, you should hunt only in secluded areas where bullets that miss the mark will do no harm. Handgunners need to be as cautious as riflemen in this respect.

Hunting with a handgun presents a real challenge, and the rewards of success are commensurate. You may not always bring game home, but when you do put dinner on the table with your handgun, you can take pride in the fact that you've beaten some long odds.

WHY TED NUGENT HUNTS WITH A HANDGUN

Ted Nugent is The New York Times *best-selling author of* God, Guns & Rock-N-Roll *and co-author with wife Shemane of* Kill It & Grill It—A Guide to Preparing and Cooking Wild Game and Fish. *Shemane also published* Married to a Rock Star *with The Lyons Press last year. An outspoken critic of gun control, Nugent is a lifelong fan of hunting and handguns. Here, he tells why handguns are enjoying such growing popularity among hunters.*

Ask any adventurer for the details of his most moving moment in the wild, and nine out of ten times it will include a close-range encounter with a wild animal. Morning coffee at the birdfeeder is fun and an important part of my life. Geese overhead always cause me to stop and smile. All animal encounters are essential for my quality of life. But the wilder the setting, the better it feels. Sometimes these stories are told by surviving witnesses because many have died at the peak of their excitement. Spiritual orgasms, if you will.

A golden glow against a mountainous backdrop is always a defining image. A soaring eagle above an endless escarpment of forever timber stirs the soul. But it is the close-up and personal dynamic of animal life in our face that will electrify man every time. Like a mega bolt of lightning straight up the kicker, there is something awe-inspiring about the presence of critters within snorting distance. The Great Spirit of the Wild is life changing when we see it beyond Disney's screen.

Great visionary men like Saxton Pope, Art Young, Fred Bear, Howard Hill, Ben Pearson, Earl Hoyt, Roy Case, Glen St. Charles, Bob Swinehart, Guy Madison, Chuck Saunders, John Mussachia, Bob Munger, Jack Howard, Jim Dougherty, Bruce Gilpin, George Nicholls, Claude Pollington, Ron Chamberlain, and so many others shared their love of nature and archery by promoting the soul-stirring invigoration of the close-range demands of the bow and arrow.

There was an undeniable, even unprecedented, excitement to their cries for the mystical flight of the arrow. Their raves about bowhunting were not about taking game, but rather, about *getting close* in order to take it. Because something bold took place on every stalk. None of these archers could get over the thrill of breaking that old hundred-yard circle of wildlife's incredible defense network, and they could not get enough of it.

The .30–30 would do just fine at one hundred yards, but at that range, the bowhunt was just beginning. The hunter would be forced to hone his stealth, stalking, woodsmanship, and natural predator skills to new heights of intensity heretofore unknown in the modern white-man hunting world. If you think buck fever is something at two or three hundred yards, try it at ten and be ready to rock. So it goes with the growth of blackpowder, old fashioned firearms of all types, and particularly the exploding interest in handgun hunting. It is not, on the average, as exacting as the bow-and-arrow maneuver, but damn close, and handgunning represents a terrific bridge from long gun to archery.

Though many handheld firearms are absolutely capable of superb accuracy well beyond the hundred-yard mark, most pistoleros pursue their sport for the get-closer challenge. My single-shot break-top T/C Contender in .375 JDJ with its 6X Leupold is a genuine three-hundred-yard banger capable of tipping over and cleanly killing anything that walks, way out there. And the related marksmanship demands associated with that are thrills unto themselves.

Developing handgun proficiency is far more demanding than long-gun work. However, my preference in handgun hunting is open-sighted arms in standard calibers that perform a variety of functions—like my old reliable S&W M29 .44 magnum and my very favorite, a stock Glock M20 semi-auto in 10mm persuasion.

Having carried a handgun all my life as a practical and essential part of responsible survival and protection for my family, I believe in having a relationship with this everyday working tool in order to have ultimate, life-and-death confidence in the weapon and my capabilities with it.

To a great degree, a hunter's responsibility is close to that self-preservation dynamic, in that, like a life-threatening encounter, a game shot is nearly always an explosion of instantaneous and spontaneous decision making. It must be a well-trained, second-nature response developed through a disciplined system of intense practice and training. There are millions and millions of dedicated handgun hunters out there, and the numbers grow every year. But one must decide to put in the long hours to get good.

It is real simple, and anyone can excel at handgunning if they are willing to put in the effort. I was lucky to have master mentors in my dad, Uncle John, and Mike and Kevin Stelling-worth, but there are so many handgun enthusiasts nowadays that good direction, knowledge, and guidance can be gained at most sporting-goods shops.

What Fred Bear is to bowhunting, Michigander Larry Kelly is to handgun hunting. This legendary man has taken every big game animal on the globe from deer, moose, all the wild sheep species, and brown bear to elephant, rhino, lion, leopard, and everything in between. He founded Mag-na-port arms, inventing and perfecting the laser-cut muzzle break recoil reduction system that changed the sporting world's attitude toward handguns as a legitimate big game hunting choice. With the help of other handgun hunting technicians like Lee Jurras, Elmer Keith, Hal Swiggett, J. D. Jones at SSK Industries, and others, handgun hunting has been made practical for everyone.

And don't think you need a special gun to have a great hunt. Many factory, out-of-the-box revolvers and autos are ready to go. The general agreement in the industry is to stick with well-constructed bullets in .40 caliber on up. The .357 magnum, though enjoyed with success by many, is in my opinion on the light side and should be limited to shots less than fifty yards under ideal circumstances—meaning the hottest loads for stationery, broadside shots on deer-sized critters on down. Nix on the .45 ACP. The .44 and .41 magnums are favorites, as well as hot 10mm, .45 long Colt, and the specialized single-shot hand cannons.

Be one of the tens of millions of law-abiding handgunners in America; take it to the next level, and go get yourself some organic dinner with a sidearm this season. Practice like mad. Breathe easy and squeeze smoothly, and get out the garlic and butter.

Chapter 1

A BRIEF HISTORY OF HANDGUNS

Handguns have fascinated man since soon after gunpowder was invented. There is considerable evidence that the Chinese were using a weak explosive compound to propel crude rockets and create fireworks early in the eleventh century. A hundred years later, the Chinese began using this early form of gunpowder to fire arrows from a reinforced bamboo tube—the first handgun.

The Mongols and Arabs later shared this secret, while in Europe both Roger Bacon and the scholar Albertus Magnus wrote of gunpowder in the mid-thirteenth century. But the first historical record of a metal gun appears in three separate documents written in the same year—1326. Two of these, written by Walter de Milemete, chaplain to King Edward III, contained drawings of vase-shaped cannons firing arrows. The third document was from Italy; it mentioned that the Florentine council ordered the construction of metal cannons with ammunition in the form of iron arrows and balls.

By the mid-fourteenth century, primitive cannons of varying size became common throughout Europe. The smallest of these were the first "handguns"—that is, they were small enough to be carried and fired in the hands of a single man. These early "one-man" guns consisted of nothing more than a short-barreled cannon attached to some kind of shaft or handle. These primitive handguns were loaded by first pouring a charge of powder down the barrel, followed by a ball of stone, iron, or lead.

To fire the gun, the shooter pointed the muzzle in the general direction he wanted the projectile to go, and then ignited the powder charge by placing a piece of glowing coal or a still-hot ember over a small hole usually drilled through the top of the barrel directly over the powder charge. This arrangement was known as the cannon lock.

This procedure was slow, uncertain, and awkward, since it often required the use of two hands to steady and aim the weapon. These small, portable hand cannons were later provided with a hook near the muzzle end. This was used to brace the gun against a wall or tree, which left a hand free to effect ignition and also served to absorb some of the gun's recoil.

While these early guns were highly unreliable and almost impossible to aim with any accuracy, they soon began to change the entire concept of warfare. Before they were developed, the armored knight was all but invulnerable to the weapons of the day. A carefully placed arrow or crossbow bolt could penetrate some types of armor, but the mounted knight had little to fear from the common soldier.

The new portable guns changed all that. These hand-operated weapons were simple and cheap to make, and little skill was required to fire them. And the bullets (or other projectiles) they fired would pierce armor. By equipping large numbers of men with these weapons, a military commander could take the initiative away from an armored and mounted foe.

These first handguns were made in a wide variety of sizes and wore any number of different stock styles. Because of their large size and method of firing, some guns were held with the handle braced firmly against the chest or tucked under an arm. Many of these hand-operated firearms more closely resembled today's rifles or shotguns than they did a pistol.

When rifles and muskets designed to be braced against the shooter's shoulder were developed, the traditional weapons of war, such as pikes, swords, and longbows, were soon abandoned. By the latter part of the sixteenth century, the longbow was very nearly obsolete.

MATCHLOCKS, WHEEL LOCKS, AND FLINTLOCKS

As more convenient firing methods were developed, firearms became less bulky and at the same time more accurate. The matchlock represented the first real advance over the original cannon lock. The matchlock used a length of slow-burning cord held in an S-shaped clamp to cause ignition. A trigger mechanism evolved to make this process even easier.

The invention of the wheel lock made firearm ignition more reliable and even simpler to control. The heart of this system was a steel wheel powered by spring pressure. The wheel revolved against a piece of pyrite to produce sparks. This resulted in even smaller, more compact firearms, including forerunners of the modern pistol.

References to wheel-lock pistols appeared as early as 1507, and improved versions continued to appear for the next 150 years. It was the wheel lock that made shooting popular as a sport. Wheel-lock firearms were widely used for hunting, and target shooting developed into a form of sporting competition.

The wheel lock made using pistols from horseback a practical tactic. The matchlock, with its ever-present length of burning cord, was too awkward to use from the saddle. There was also the danger of having that sputtering cord accidentally come in contact with the horse, with predictably unfortunate results.

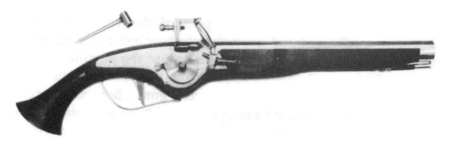

The invention of the wheel lock made smaller, more compact handguns possible, leading to the development of the first practical pistol. Wheel-lock pistols appeared as early as 1507.

With the invention of the wheel lock, multiple-shot handguns began to appear. Guns with two, three, and four barrels were made, and during the late sixteenth century some unknown genius devised the first revolver: a wheel-lock handgun with a revolving cylinder behind a single barrel. Like the modern revolver, that early repeater held six loaded chambers that could be moved into place in turn. The cylinder had to be rotated by hand, and the single priming pan had to be refilled with fine powder before every shot, but the operating principle remained the same.

The snaphance and its successor, the flintlock, eventually made the wheel lock obsolete. The flintlock was a simpler, more reliable mechanism that struck a piece of flint against a curving steel plate when its trigger was pulled. The resulting sparks were directed downward into a powder-filled pan. This rapidly burning powder then ignited the main powder charge contained in the base of the bore.

The snaphance made its appearance around 1556, while the first true flintlock came on the scene a half-century later. Because the flintlock was simpler than the wheel lock, it was cheaper and easier to manufacture. Some early matchlocks were later converted into flintlocks, and by the beginning of the eighteenth century all armies were equipped with flintlock muskets. The flintlock pistol became the standard sidearm of travelers.

Dueling pistols evolved into the accepted means used by gentlemen to settle important differences. During the late eighteenth century, these pistols became so fashionable that they were considered a required part of every gentleman's possessions.

With the introduction of the relatively inexpensive flintlock, rifles and handguns began enjoying much wider use. Pistols were frequently supplied in pairs and were used by men and women alike. Also, the widespread availability of reliable and affordable pistols and long guns soon made shooting a highly popular sport. What had once been a defensive or offensive weapon became a tool for relaxation and enjoyment.

Although flintlock guns represented a major stride forward, they were far from perfect. Because ignition depended on sparks finding and igniting priming powder held in a pan, which in turn fired the main powder charge, misfires were a regular occurrence. This complicated firing chain also caused an appreciable delay from the time the trigger was pulled until the gun actually fired. Also, the system was vulnerable to wet or windy weather.

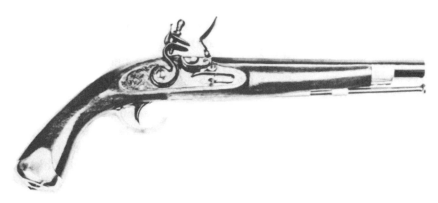

Cheaper and easier to manufacture, flintlock guns made the wheel lock obsolete.

PERCUSSION HANDGUNS

The Reverend Alexander Forsyth changed all that when he began using fulminate compounds, which could be detonated by a sharp blow, to ignite the main propellant powder charge. His discovery led to the development of the percussion lock, and eventually to the cartridge guns we still use today.

Until the self-contained cartridge, with its own percussion cap, or primer, completely revolutionized the arms-making trade, percussion-lock guns ruled the roost. Many flintlock guns were soon converted to the new percussion firing system, and many new guns were designed. The copper percussion cap, which was placed on a nipple over the firing chamber and struck by a hammer to cause ignition, was much more convenient and reliable than all preceding systems.

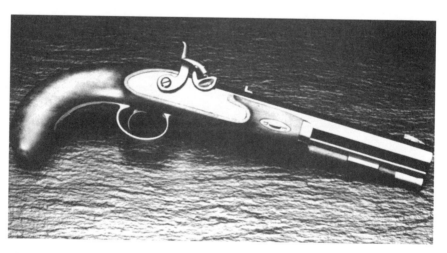

The percussion cap, invented by the Reverend Alexander Forsyth, led the way to the development of the percussion lock, which was much more reliable and convenient than the flintlock.

MULTIPLE-BARRELED AND
MODERN REPEATING HANDGUNS

Multiple-barreled pepperboxes and other repeating pistols soon appeared, but it wasn't until Samuel Colt designed his now famous single-action revolver that the first truly practical repeating handgun became available. The first Colt patents were issued in 1835, and after a shaky start, Colt's gun company began to flourish with the production of the large Walker Colt in 1847. American troops were issued these handguns during the Mexican War, marking the first widespread military use of revolvers.

While Colt's revolvers were earning an impressive reputation in this country, John and Philip Webley began producing percussion revolvers of their own design in Great Britain as early as 1833. The British government eventually adopted the rugged Webley in 1887, and this famous handgun has since seen service in every part of the globe.

Similarly, Horace Smith and Daniel Wesson began producing a seven-shot .22-caliber revolver in 1857. Thirteen years later, their company began manufacturing a .44 revolver that was adopted by the Russian government. This was the first large-caliber American cartridge revolver. It was followed by Colt's famed single-action .45 in 1873. This revolver—the Single-Action Army Model—is probably the most famous handgun of all time. Copies of this venerable weapon are still in production, and millions remain in use today.

"Buffalo Bill" Cody and others used Colt revolvers in extravagantly staged displays of shooting and horsemanship around the turn of the century, and Western movies continue to keep the single-action Colt in the public eye.

The Single-Action Shooting Society (S.A.S.S.) stages old-time shooting matches all around the country. Participants dress

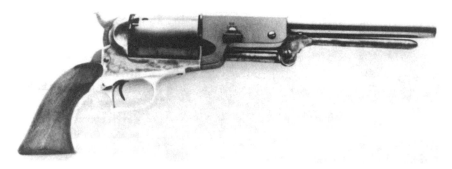

The first commercially successful revolver was the Walker model Colt introduced in 1847. This big percussion handgun was the forerunner of the modern revolver.

Colt's Single-Action Army Model .45, a cartridge gun developed from the earlier percussion Colt designs, is likely the most famous handgun of all time.

in period clothing, and only nineteenth-century guns (or modern replicas) are allowed. Single-action revolvers made by Colt, Ruger, the United States Firearms Manufacturing Company, and gunmakers in other countries see a lot of use during these events. Few handguns have such widespread appeal and readily invoke such nostalgia.

Another famous handgun, the John M. Browning–designed Model 1911 Colt auto pistol, has served the U.S. military as a sidearm since before the First World War. In addition to its uses as a military weapon, this gun has proven to be a finely accurate target pistol when properly tuned and fitted. The U.S. military has now replaced the single-action 1911A1, which fired .45 ACP

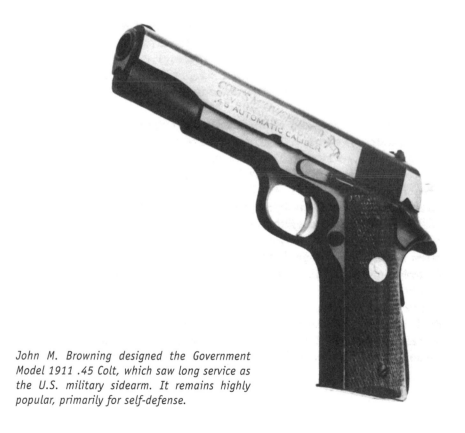

John M. Browning designed the Government Model 1911 .45 Colt, which saw long service as the U.S. military sidearm. It remains highly popular, primarily for self-defense.

(Automatic Colt Pistol) ammunition, with a double-action Beretta that digests the 9mm ammo used by other NATO forces.

While the 1911 has been retired from active duty, it's more popular than ever with civilian shooters. Kimber, Springfield Armory, Colt, Smith & Wesson, Dan Wesson, and a variety of other manufacturers are turning out 1911A1 pistols in record numbers.

New, stronger, more powerful revolvers are being developed specifically for hunters. (These are covered in depth in chapter 4.) Similarly, a variety of optical sighting systems—again primarily designed with hunters in mind—are now available for pistols and revolvers. These advancements were unheard of a half-century ago. (Handgun sights are discussed in chapter 5.)

Advances continue to be made in handgun design and manufacture, and many of the models offered today represent vast improvements over those available only a decade or so ago. More powerful cartridges continue to be introduced, along with superstrong handguns to digest them.

Once considered little more than a novelty, hunting with handguns is rapidly growing in popularity. Sportsmen and women who elect to hunt with iron-sighted (not scoped) revolvers typically stalk within forty or fifty yards before attempting a shot.

Handgunners can successfully take game at much longer ranges if they use a scope-equipped pistol chambering a flat-shooting cartridge. Skilled shooters kill prairie dogs cleanly at three hundred yards and more. Their specialized guns are capable of rifle-like accuracy and performance.

The history of handguns is still being written, and hunters are providing many of the most recent chapters. Once used primarily for law enforcement, military service, and self-defense, handguns are now regarded as a fun, effective, legitimate sporting tool.

Chapter 2

THE BASICS:
AUTO PISTOLS,
REVOLVERS, OR
SINGLE SHOTS

All handguns fit one of two categories: pistols or revolvers. Each has its own features and advantages, as well as its own distinctive handling qualities. Pistols include single-shot and autoloading handguns—flat-sided selfloaders featuring a reciprocating slide or bolt and fed by a spring-loaded magazine. All have hunting applications. Although most auto pistols are designed for target shooting or self-defense, a few—notably Magnum Research's big Desert Eagle chambered for rounds like the .44 magnum and the even more potent .50 Action Express (A.E.)—are well suited for hunting deer and larger game. Rimfire auto pistols are great for squirrel and rabbit hunting.

Revolvers are multiple-shot handguns with a revolving cylinder at the rear of the barrel. This cylinder typically contains from five to nine individual firing chambers, which are rotated into alignment with the bore for firing. The sixguns you see in Western movies are revolvers. A few decades ago, most uniformed

Autoloaders are slab-sided pistols fed by removable spring-loaded magazines.

Revolvers feature a revolving cylinder behind the barrel. The cylinder contains from five to nine individual firing chambers, which rotate to line up with the bore.

policemen wore revolvers to work. But that's all changed. Now, nearly all law enforcement officers in the country are issued auto pistols with high-capacity magazines. Auto pistols are also favored by target shooters and have long been *de rigueur* for military forces worldwide.

The modern single-shot pistol—many shooting high-intensity loads in interchangeable barrels of different calibers—is a relatively new development. Most modern single-shot pistols are hunting guns, pure and simple. By far the most popular single-shot pistols on the market are the Thompson/Center Contender, which has been with us for more than thirty years, and its higher-powered sibling, the Encore. These T/C centerfires and other long-barreled pistols chamber rifle ammunition or extremely potent handgun fodder, making long-range kills possible for skilled handgun hunters. These single-shot pistols are bulky, and the lack of fast follow-up shots precludes the one-shooter from serious antisocial use.

Single-shot pistols like the Thompson/Center Contender chamber flat-shooting cartridges and may have an effective hunting range of two hundred yards or more.

DOUBLE ACTION VERSUS SINGLE ACTION

To further complicate handgun taxonomy, revolvers and auto pistols are divided into double-action and single-action types. Single-action guns must be manually cocked before they can be fired; double-action types can be fired by simply pulling the trigger.

If you don't have an owner's manual or some other identifying literature for your handgun, the only way to determine if a particular auto pistol is a single action or double action is to see if simply pulling the trigger makes the hammer fall (you'll hear a distinct metallic "click"). Before you try this, be sure the gun is unloaded and pointing in a safe direction.

Some auto pistols have an external hammer visible at the rear of the gun. If this hammer is resting all the way forward, the gun is uncocked. Move the safety lever to the "off safe" position, point the gun at the ground, or in some other safe direction, and pull the trigger. If the hammer rises and falls, the gun operates in

You must manually cock a single-action revolver before firing.

the double-action mode. If the hammer must be manually cocked—either by pulling the slide all the way to the rear and releasing it or by thumbing the hammer all the way back—before the trigger can be pulled, you have a single-action handgun.

But with auto pistols, this distinction holds true for the first shot only. Once the gun is fired, the action automatically ejects the empty cartridge case, cocks itself, and chambers a fresh round. From that point onward, you need only pull the trigger to continue shooting until the magazine is empty.

If an auto pistol's hammer or striker is concealed within the action, you can determine whether it's a double-action or single-action gun by pulling the trigger twice. If the gun was originally cocked—which will be the case if you opened the action (as advised) to make sure no live rounds remained in the chamber or magazine—pulling the trigger once will cause the firing pin to click against the empty chamber. This uncocks the gun. If the striker/firing-pin mechanism fails to click again the second time you pull the trigger, the pistol is single action. This test is usually made with the safety in the "off" position, so be absolutely certain the gun is pointed in a direction that would cause no harm or danger if it should somehow fire.

Keeping guns pointed in a safe direction at all times—and particularly when you're testing the trigger—is a rule that will absolutely, positively prevent accidental shootings. It's a rule all experienced shooters invariably follow.

As for revolvers, single actions must be manually cocked by thumbing the hammer back before firing. Most single-action revolvers are identified by their distinctive "western" look, including a long hammer spur and gracefully curving plowhandle-shaped grips. Another tip-off is the long ejector-rod housing located beneath the barrel, but offset to one side. On double-action revolvers, the ejector rod is directly under the barrel, not offset.

Single-action revolvers are loaded (and unloaded) through a small, hinged gate found in the recoil shield on the right side of the gun. The recoil shield is the smoothly rounded projection located immediately behind the cylinder. When the hinged gate is opened and the gun's hammer either fully lowered or placed at half cock (depending on model), the cylinder

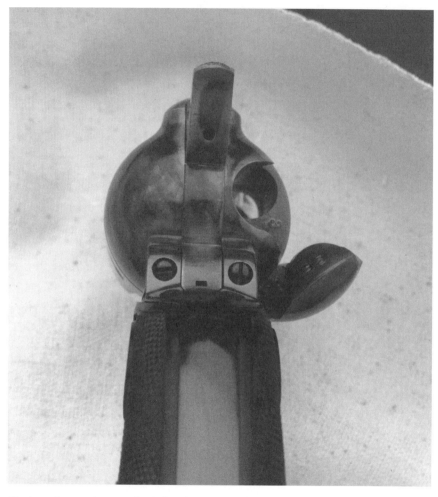

Single-action revolvers are loaded and unloaded through a hinged gate in the recoil shield on the right side of the gun.

Double-action revolvers feature cylinders that swing to one side for reloading.

can be manually rotated to bring each firing chamber in line with the gate. Ammunition can then be inserted or removed from each chamber.

But beware: Original single-action Colts and most modern replicas have fixed firing pins protruding from the face of the hammer. These revolvers, when loaded, can only be carried safely if an empty chamber lies under the lowered hammer. This means loading only five chambers and leaving the sixth vacant—then making sure that chamber is in line with the bore when you holster the gun. Modern single-action wheelguns from Ruger, Magnum Research, and Freedom Arms that sport floating firing pins and automatic safeties can be safely carried with all chambers fully stoked.

Nearly all double-action revolvers are loaded by first disengaging the cylinder crane latch located on the left side of the handgun, then moving the cylinder to the left to expose all the firing chambers. Pressing the ejector rod to the rear ejects live loads or fired cases from all chambers simultaneously. The cylinder can then be reloaded and clicked back into place.

PISTOLS VERSUS REVOLVERS

Single-action revolvers are slower to reload than double actions. Also, you must manually cock the hammer of a single-action six-gun each and every time you shoot. This isn't a problem for handgun hunters, who usually cock double-action revolvers before making the first shot anyway. Manually cocking the hammer results in a shorter, lighter trigger pull that makes accurate shooting much easier. However, you can obviously get follow-up shots off a lot quicker with a double-action revolver.

Single-shot pistols like the Contender and Encore are chambered for very fast, flat-shooting cartridges and are capable of surprising accuracy. They're favored by an increasing number of hunting sportsmen, particularly those who intend to mount a scope and shoot at distances longer than seventy-five yards. Metallic-silhouette target shooters also buy and use these specialized one-shooters.

Thompson/Center's single-shot pistols feature interchangeable barrels, enabling the user to shoot a variety of different cartridges and calibers in the same firearm. This gives these guns a degree of versatility unmatched in any other handgun type. Limitations include low rate of fire. The gun must be opened, cleared of the fired cartridge case, reloaded, closed, and cocked before you can follow up with a second shot. And most single-shot pistols are large and bulky, making them less convenient to carry holstered than revolvers or auto pistols.

In spite of their disadvantages, one-shooters are an ideal choice for hunters who want the ultimate in range and accuracy from a flat-shooting, high-velocity load. They're willing to forgo rapid re-

Single-action auto pistols typically feature one or more manually operated safeties, a slide stop, and a magazine release button.

peat shots and carrying ease.

To achieve optimum velocities, most single-shot pistols sport fairly long barrels. Ten inches is a popular length, and some models are available with twelve- and fourteen-inch tubes. Expanding gases push the bullet through the bore, and the longer the barrel, the greater the velocity. Long-barreled handguns also offer long sighting planes when used with iron sights, which reduces aiming error. This isn't a factor if a scope is mounted, but a long-barreled gun is always easier to steady on target than a short-barreled firearm.

The Savage Striker is a bolt-action pistol with a magazine that, when necessary, makes fast follow-up shots possible. It doesn't feature interchangeable barrels, but it's offered in a handful of high-intensity rifle chamberings. Until a few years ago, Remington and Weatherby also produced long-range bolt pistols. Sadly, these excellent guns have been discontinued.

Revolvers and auto pistols are offered in barrel lengths varying from two to ten inches—sometimes more. Stubby two-inch tubes aren't much use to sportsmen; they deliver increased muzzle blast and recoil, along with a lot less *oomph*. They're also lacking in accuracy. Most hunters use handguns with six-inch or longer barrels. Four-inch barrels are more compact and easy to carry holstered, but a 6- or 7½-inch tube offers better handling (and aiming) characteristics. A handgun with a barrel at least six inches long generally points better, recoils less, and delivers a milder report. Longer barrels also mean higher velocities, which translate into increased power. That's why many state hunting regulations stipulate that handguns must have barrels at least six inches long.

Revolvers with 7½- or 8-inch barrels may require a shoulder holster. Some belt holsters accommodate an eight-inch barrel, but drawing a handgun from such rigs is awkward at best. The shoulder holster keeps the handgun tucked high under the shooter's armpit, where it's safely out of the way until time to

The long barrel on this T/C Contender pistol delivers maximum velocity.

Auto pistols automatically eject fired casings, often throwing them several yards into the air.

shoot. If your handgun wears a scope, a shoulder or across-the-chest bandoleer-type holster may be your best option.

Revolvers and auto pistols differ in one other important aspect. Autoloaders almost always have some kind of manual safety that locks either trigger or firing pin, or both. This safety is usually a thumb lever found on the left side of the slide or receiver. The gun is normally carried with the safety in the "on safe" position. The lever must be returned to the "fire" position before the pistol will shoot.

In contrast, nearly all revolvers lack any kind of manual safety, although many incorporate some kind of hammer safety or transfer bar that prevents firing unless the trigger is depressed.

On the plus side, revolvers are considerably less fussy about the ammo they're fed, while autoloaders may balk with substandard loads. If a revolver fails to fire, pulling the trigger again rotates the cylinder and puts a fresh round under the hammer.

If you are a reloader, revolvers retain expended cartridges the shooter can eject at leisure. Autoloaders throw cases several feet away, often into tall grass or brush. For hunters, though, a much more important consideration is that revolvers are able to digest much heavier, more potent loads than most auto pistols. This makes the magnum revolver the first choice of many hunting handgunners.

Auto pistols, single shots, and revolvers each have advocates. They all have advantages and disadvantages, and individual shooters have their own ideas about what makes the perfect hunting handgun. (Before making your choice, check out chapter 4, where you'll find more detailed information on the pros and cons of specific handgun types and hunting cartridges.)

Chapter 3

SHOOTING HANDGUNS SAFELY AND ACCURATELY

THE BASICS

It takes a lot of practice and patience to learn to shoot a handgun well, but the basics can be grasped in a single session. Some beginners find they have a natural knack for handgunning and quickly develop the skills necessary to put their bullets on target. Others learn more slowly, but the fact is that almost anyone can achieve a fair degree of proficiency with a handgun.

Of the three basic firearm types—rifle, handgun, and shotgun—the handgun is the most difficult to shoot well. When plinking or practicing at targets, handguns are typically held at arm's length and steadied only by the shooter's hands (*both* hands). In contrast, rifles and shotguns have full-length stocks that can be snugged to the shooter's shoulder, offering a high degree of steady support. When hunting, both riflemen and handgunners take advantage of external field supports every chance they get. Because pistols and revolvers are so doggone hard to hold still, a solid shooting position and some kind of steadying support are vital to hunting handgunners.

Recoil is transmitted primarily to the rifleman's (or shotgunner's) shoulder, and rubber recoil pads can help ease the shock. But a handgunner receives all the recoil forces in the palm of his shooting hand. In addition, the factory sights furnished on most handguns have a very short sighting radius, magnifying the effect of aiming errors and making pinpoint accuracy much more difficult. Even scope-sighted handguns are more difficult to aim than a similarly equipped rifle.

It takes muscle control and hours of practice to hold a handgun steady on target for the few fleeting seconds needed to trigger an accurate shot. Holding two or three pounds of dead weight at arm's length tires muscles in a hurry. You must hold the gun very still while you line up the sights, and then maintain that static pose while you carefully squeeze the trigger. Learning to do this consistently takes time and practice.

Rifles have full-length stocks that can be snugged against the shooter's shoulder for support. Handguns are steadied by hands alone.

Holding a two- or three-pound deadweight at arm's length becomes tiring in a hurry.

SAFETY STEPS THAT PREVENT ACCIDENTS

The first and most important thing a beginning handgunner needs to learn is safety. An entire chapter will be devoted to safety rules later on in the book (see chapter 15), but the basics can be quickly memorized.

1. Treat every gun as if it were loaded.
2. Watch that muzzle!
3. Never point a gun at anything you don't intend to shoot.
4. Always be sure of your target and backstop.
5. Immediately open the action and inspect for live ammunition when you pick up a gun.
6. Keep guns unloaded when not in use.
7. Be sure the barrel is clear of obstruction before firing.
8. Never shoot at a hard, flat surface or water. Ricochets can result.

9. Store guns and ammunition separately, locked safely out of reach of children.

10. Don't mix alcohol and gunpowder.

HOW TO CLEAR AND INSPECT HANDGUNS

In order to follow safety rules five, six, and seven above you must first learn how to safely check for ammunition in the actions of auto pistols, single shots, and revolvers.

To clear and inspect the action of an auto pistol, hold the grip in your shooting hand, point the muzzle skyward, and use your free hand to remove the magazine from its recess in the butt. The magazine-release catch will usually be located in the left grip somewhere behind and/or below the trigger guard or in the base of the butt. Be sure to keep your finger off the trigger during this exercise.

Watch that muzzle! When carrying a handgun, never allow it to point anywhere but in a safe direction.

Next, use your free hand to pull the slide rearward. If a live round is chambered, it should automatically eject as the slide travels back. If the gun has a locking lever, the slide can then be locked in the open position. Visually check the chamber at this point to make sure it's clear of ammo. Leave the magazine out and the slide open until you're ready to shoot. Then you only need to replace the loaded magazine. If the slide doesn't move forward when the magazine clicks home, simply pull the slide to the rear and release it or depress the locking lever. As it returns to battery, the slide will automatically strip a cartridge from the magazine and feed it to the chamber. The gun is then ready to fire.

Once the auto pistol is cocked and loaded (cycling the slide automatically cocks the action), the safety lever should be engaged until you're ready to fire. Again, keep that muzzle pointed straight up, at the ground, or safely downrange at all times.

To inspect the chambers of a double-action revolver, simply press the cylinder-release catch (located on the left side of the frame) and use your other hand to crane the cylinder to the left as far as it will go. Once the cylinder is clear of the frame the gun cannot fire, even if the cylinder is fully loaded with live ammunition. The gun can then be safely carried by grasping the top strap, with your fingers inside the opening that the cylinder formerly occupied. The gun should be carried butt forward, with the cylinder fully extended from the frame.

If you don't intend to shoot the gun immediately, it can be rendered even safer by removing the loads from their chambers. Pointing the muzzle upward will allow unfired rounds to fall from the cylinder into your waiting hand.

If you intend to carry your double-action revolver loaded and holstered, make sure it's uncocked. To uncock a revolver, first point the muzzle in a safe direction (downrange or at the ground). Then hold the hammer back with your thumb while you gently depress the trigger. While keeping the trigger depressed, use your thumb to carefully and gently lower the hammer all the way forward. Most double-action revolvers have no external safety levers, but may be safely carried with the hammer resting against a loaded chamber.

Single-action revolvers require a different procedure for clearing and checking. Their cylinders are held in place by a center pin, and the cylinder can't be simply craned to one side. The only way to check these guns and make sure no live rounds are chambered is to visually inspect each chamber one by one. This is done by first pulling the hammer back to half cock, then opening the loading

gate on the right-side recoil shield. (The hammer needn't be drawn back on late-model Ruger single-action revolvers. Simply opening the loading gate unlocks the cylinder on these guns.)

Manually rotate the cylinder to bring each chamber into view through the loading gate. Count the chambers and make sure all six are empty. As before, the muzzle

Breaking the action allows you to load or check the chamber of some single-shot pistols.

should be kept pointing in a safe direction while you perform this check.

If any cartridges remain in their chambers, they can be removed by pulling the ejector-rod stud (located on the left side and underneath the barrel near the gun's muzzle) back toward the cylinder while the loaded chamber is in direct line with the loading gate. Remove all cartridge cases, even if they've been fired. The gun can't be considered safe until all chambers are empty. Even then, the gun should be accorded the same care and respect you'd give a loaded firearm.

SINGLE-ACTION SIXGUN SAFETY RULES

Unless your single-action wheelgun features a modern hammer-block or transfer-bar safety lever, it should be loaded with only five rounds. The gun should then be carried with the hammer down over the empty chamber. Loading one chamber of an empty cylinder, rotating the cylinder to skip the next chamber, loading the remaining four chambers, then gently lowering the hammer should accomplish this. Old-style single-action guns have fixed firing pins that rest directly against the cartridge primer when the hammer is lowered against a loaded chamber. A sharp blow to the exposed hammer can easily cause an accidental discharge. Newer designs, like those featured on Ruger's New Model Blackhawk and similar guns, feature rebounding firing pins and hammer-block safeties. They can safely be carried fully loaded, with the hammer down over an unfired cartridge.

It's possible to remove the cylinder from single-action sixguns for added safety during transportation or storage. Simply depress the cylinder pin lock (located in the frame immediately ahead of the cylinder), and while keeping the lock depressed, pull the cylinder pin toward the muzzle as far as it will go. Open the loading gate (in the recoil shield on the right side of the frame), then push the cylinder to the right until it's clear of the gun.

To check the chamber of a break-top single-shot pistol, unlock the action according to the instructions accompanying your gun and pull down on the barrel until the chamber is bared for inspection.

DO YOUR HOMEWORK BEFORE SHOOTING

Regardless of the type of handgun you're using, you should carefully read the owner's manual accompanying it and become thoroughly acquainted with the gun's operation before you ever attempt to load it or take it to the shooting range. Make sure you know where the safety catches and the magazine-release and slide-release levers are located on an auto pistol, or become familiar with the location and operation of the cylinder release and ejector assembly on your revolver. Every make and model

Good eye and ear protection are important whenever you shoot a handgun—particularly on the practice range.

differs at least slightly from the next, and it's your responsibility to know how to operate your own gun safely.

Once you know how to operate your handgun, it's time to head to the shooting range. Before you go, there are some additional purchases that must be made. First, you need a supply of ammunition—make sure the cartridges you buy are the proper loads for your gun. The correct cartridge designation should be stamped on the barrel or slide of your handgun, usually on the left side. Buy only cartridges carrying this same designation.

You also need some kind of ear protection. Ear protectors are discussed at length in chapter 15, but they basically fall into two categories: earplugs or earmuff-type cups that cover the entire ear. The earmuff-type protectors are more effective and usually more comfortable than earplugs. Either type can be purchased at any sporting-goods store or gun counter. Without adequate ear protection, you won't shoot nearly as well—and you'll enjoy shooting far less. More importantly, shooting without taking these precautions will definitely cause permanent damage to your hearing.

Shooting glasses are another recommended accessory. Handguns may spit small bits of lead or cartridge casings back in your face, and hardened eyeglass lenses are cheap insurance against possible injury. Even if you're not using a centerfire handgun, it's important to wear protective lenses. I've had my face peppered more than once when a low-powered .22 rimfire cartridge case failed. A tiny bit of metal or burnt powder can cause serious eye damage.

ASSUMING THE TARGET STANCE

The next step is learning the proper grip and stance. While some handgunners still use the formal one-handed target stance, most experienced shooters prefer a two-handed pose. These handgunners range from casual plinkers to police officers—and most definitely hunters.

To assume the once popular classic target stance, a right-handed shooter grips the gun solidly in his right hand, faces anywhere from forty-five to eighty degrees away from the target, and plants his feet a comfortable distance apart. He then extends the gun at arm's length, pointing toward the target. The arm is held straight out at shoulder height, and the shooter views his sights over his right shoulder. The left hand is placed in a pocket or on the left hip or simply allowed to dangle.

This stance is still used in some forms of target competition. However, it's a very unsteady position, and it's not the best choice for a beginning shooter. Hunters and other sportsmen almost never rely on it.

The two-handed hold is much steadier, and a great deal more practical. Both hands support the gun's weight, and you face the target squarely. To shoot two-handed, first grasp the grip firmly in the shooting hand. The heel of the hand should be in direct contact with the backstrap, and the hand should be positioned as high as possible on the grip. If you're shooting an auto pistol, the web between your thumb and forefinger should be pressed firmly against the upper curve of the backstrap.

The fingers should be wrapped snugly around the grip. The tip of the index, or trigger, finger should contact the trigger face when firing a single action. To control the heavier double-action trigger pull, you may have to use the first joint of your finger to gain the necessary leverage. The thumb should point forward along the grip on the side opposite your knuckles.

The supporting hand should wrap around the shooting hand, with the fingers overlapping. The index finger of the supporting hand can wrap in front of, or immediately under, the trigger guard. Never use two fingers on the trigger itself. The thumb of the sup-

Handguns should be firmly gripped in the shooting hand, with the supporting hand overlapping.

port hand should point forward along the same side of the grip if you're using an auto pistol. With a revolver, you can wrap this thumb over the thumb web of the shooting hand if you prefer. Just don't try this variation with an auto pistol in your hands or the slide may chew off a chunk of flesh as it cycles rearward under recoil.

After firmly gripping the gun in the two-handed hold, face the target with your feet spread a comfortable distance apart. If you shoot right-handed, your left foot should be slightly closer to the target. Next, stand erect and hold the gun directly in front of you. The right arm should be extended straight toward the target, while the left (supporting) arm should be slightly bent at the elbow. The left shoulder should be slightly back to help apply stabilizing pressure to the shooting hand. Hold the gun vertically, as canting it to either side (as you sometimes see in action movies filmed by someone who should know better) will cause you to miss the target.

SIGHT ALIGNMENT

Hold the gun at eye level and look along your outstretched shooting arm to align the sights. Remember to focus on the sights—primarily the front sight—and not the target. It is extremely difficult for young eyes—and impossible for old ones—to rapidly switch focus from rear sight, to front sight, to target. In a handgunner's imperfect world, *something* has to look blurry. Don't let it be the front sight.

The front sight should be evenly centered in the rear sighting notch, with an equal band of light showing on either side. The top of the front sight should be even with the shoulders of the rear sight, and the target should appear to "sit" atop the front sight blade. That's the alignment you need to hit the target. That being said, when it's time to trip the trigger, concentrate on that front sight.

Cock your handgun, align the sights on target, firm your grip, stiffen your arms, disengage the safety (if your gun has one),

Hold the gun at eye level to align front and rear sights. On the target range, focus on the front sight and let the target blur.

and carefully squeeze the trigger. Remember to don your shooting glasses and ear protection before firing that first shot. Otherwise, you can count on flinching in response to the muzzle blast, making a clean miss.

SHOOTING POSITIONS

While the two-handed standing position is the one most often used, other shooting positions provide more stability. The sitting position is steady and very comfortable. To shoot from this handy position, first sit facing the target. Bend both knees and bring them up to a comfortable level, then lean forward with the gun in the basic two-handed hold described above. Let the upper part of your arms (just behind the elbows) rest on your knees. Don't place your elbows directly on your knees, which quickly becomes uncomfortable and makes for shakier support. Extend the gun a comfortable distance in front of you, aim, and fire.

A two-handed hold and a solid shooting position are important elements of handgun hunting accuracy.

The kneeling position is also useful afield, although it's less comfortable than the sitting position. A right-handed shooter simply kneels on his right knee and places his left elbow just forward of the upraised left kneecap. Again, a two-handed grip is used, although the left supporting hand may be cupped underneath the shooting hand rather than mirroring the grip of the shooting hand.

To shoot from the prone position, lie on your stomach, facing the target and with your knees spread a comfortable distance apart. Extend both arms in line with the body, while you rest your elbows against the ground. Raise the gun to eye level, and you're ready to shoot. The prone position is very steady, but offers limited visibility in any but the lowest underbrush. It's also difficult to maintain for any length of time, as neck muscles quickly tire.

USING EXTERNAL RESTS AND SUPPORTS

Hunters and other handgunners who are serious about hitting a mark beyond point-blank range quickly learn to use external supports to help steady their guns. The basic two-handed hold is still used, but the hands are rested on or against sandbags, boulders, tree trunks, fenceposts, or any other available support. The gun itself should never come in direct contact with any hard, unyielding surface because the bullet is likely to be jarred off course. When using a relatively soft support like a sandbag the butt can safely rest against it. But when tree trunks or other hard surfaces are employed, make sure only the hands directly support the gun. Your hands should form a soft buffer between the gun and any solid surface used to steady it.

When shooting hard-kicking magnums from a field rest, it's wise to wear leather gloves to prevent skin abrasions. Without such protection, a hard-recoiling handgun will rub your hand—hard—against the unyielding support, and the results are often painful.

Bipods or shooting sticks make ideal rests for handgun hunters. Supports like Stoney Point's Steady-Stix weigh next to nothing and collapse into a compact package that can be tucked into a pocket or hung from your belt. When you're ready to shoot, it takes only seconds to deploy a Steady-Stix bipod.

The take-apart sections are strung together on shock cords. Simply give the bipod a shake, and it's pretty well self-assembling. The upper "V" of the bipod is padded, so you can rest the barrel or frame of your handgun directly against this support. These bipods can be quickly and easily adjusted to use from prone, kneeling, or sitting positions. Taller versions are available if you want to shoot standing up. The standing position isn't very steady, even with the help of a support, but in tall grass or high cover it may be your only option.

When I shoot a handgun at extended range (for me, that's anything more than forty or fifty yards), ninety percent of the time I'll haul out my bipod and drop to the sitting position. I can assume this position quickly, and I find it extremely comfortable. It also places gun and sights high enough to see over low brush. Shooting from prone—even with the aid of a bipod—soon strains the muscles in my neck.

I seldom hunt without one of these handy devices, whether I'm using a rifle or a handgun. Some handgunners are skillful and steady enough to consistently hit the vitals of deer-sized game offhand at one hundred yards, but I'm not there yet, so I depend heavily on these light, handy field rests. A variety of other portable, inexpensive shooting aids is also available.

Once you've learned how to hold and shoot your handgun comfortably, don't make the mistake of spending all your time plinking tin cans or other tempting "fun" targets. Shoot regularly at paper targets. You can buy commercially printed targets or make your own by inking a three- or four-inch circle on a sheet of

External supports like this Steady-Stix bipod are vital for shooting at long-range game.

paper. Begin shooting at fifteen yards and gradually move the targets back to twenty-five yards as your skill and confidence grow. For handgunning out to one hundred yards with iron sights, an eight-inch bull's-eye is easier to see.

Shooting at paper lets you see exactly where your shots are going and gives you some clue as to how you're progressing. With time and practice, the size of your groups will shrink. Before long, you should regularly be hitting the bull's-eye. Shooting at tin cans lets you know only that you've hit or missed the target. And when you miss, you can't measure exactly how far your bullet was from the mark or whether it's striking high, low, or to one side.

Shooting at paper targets helps discipline your eye and lets you know exactly how skillful you've become. So how skillful do you need to be? Before hunting deer-sized game at one hundred yards, you should learn to consistently group your shots into a six- or eight-inch circle at that distance. Once you can hit a paper plate with every shot, you're ready to hunt.

You needn't confine your practice to the target range, though. You can work to improve your stance and trigger control by dry firing your unloaded gun indoors. First, double-check to make sure no live ammunition remains in the firing chamber(s), cylinder, or magazine. Then cock the gun, aim it at a distant object, and carefully squeeze the trigger.

Even though you've double- or even triple-checked and *know* the gun is empty, you must respect the safety rules by pointing the gun only in a direction that would cause no injury to another person if it should somehow fire. Remember to always treat any gun as if it is loaded.

Dry firing won't hurt most handguns, although it may be advisable to insert empty .22 cartridge cases into the chambers of some .22 rimfire revolvers. Otherwise, the firing pin may eventu-

During practice, don't just plink at tin cans. Shooting at paper targets lets you know exactly where your bullets are going.

ally suffer as it strikes against the outer edge of the chamber. The empty .22 cases will buffer the firing pin and prevent such damage.

While dry firing can help train muscles and trigger fingers, the best way to practice is at the shooting range with live ammunition. Flinching will invariably make you miss what you're shooting at, so guard against this. To learn whether or not you're flinching, have a friend load your gun while you look away. If the gun is a revolver, he can leave one or two chambers empty; an auto pistol can be cocked without chambering a live round. Then go ahead and fire at the target without first checking to make sure the chamber is loaded. If your hand jerks as the hammer falls on the empty chamber, you've got a problem.

Flinching is difficult to detect when firing a loaded gun because the jerking motion is lost under recoil. Only when the hammer falls on an unloaded chamber will the flinching become easy to spot.

Before going forth on your first handgun hunt, diligently practice shooting at various distances from sitting, kneeling, and supported positions. I try to use some kind of external support any time I shoot game at anything beyond point-blank range.

A final word of advice: If possible, learn to shoot with a .22 rimfire handgun, and wait until you're proficient before graduating to one of the harder-kicking centerfires. And don't keep shooting until you're tired of practicing. Once you begin to flag, your accuracy falls off rapidly and it's easy to become discouraged. Prolonged shooting sessions take much of the fun from the sport and make you less eager to return to the range for follow-up sessions later on. Quit while you're still having fun. After all, fun is what handguns and hunting are all about.

Chapter 4

CHOOSING A HUNTING HANDGUN

Now that we've discussed the types of handguns available and the basic principles of shooting and safety, let's take a closer look at which handguns actually work best for hunting, along with the hunting cartridges they chamber.

HUNTING REVOLVERS

For many years, my favorite handgun was an early Ruger Super Blackhawk revolver. The big single-action sixgun wore a 7½-inch barrel and iron sights and digested .44 magnum ammo. I'd been warned about the .44 magnum's "ferocious recoil." After firing several full-house magnum loads through my new Ruger, I was pleasantly surprised to learn that its hard-kicking reputation was largely undeserved. The gun's extra heft helped, and its plowhandle grip let the revolver rotate upward in my hand under recoil.

The first deer I ever took with a handgun fell to a 240-grain .44 magnum factory load from that Super Blackhawk revolver. I waited in ambush alongside a recently used deer trail. When the buck ambled by, I fired one shot from a solid sitting position at a range of thirty-five paces. The animal took a couple of stumbling steps and went down. From that moment on, I was hooked on .44 magnums.

Other .44 magnums I own include a Ruger Redhawk, a six-inch S&W Model 629, a four-inch Model 629 S&W Mountain Gun, and a Dan Wesson revolver with a pair of interchangeable barrels and shrouds. A Leupold scope rides on one shroud, while the other sports a Bushnell Holosight.

The Holosight and other red-dot sights work well on hunting handguns. They're faster than open sights or long-eye-relief scopes, and when mounted on pistols shooting high-intensity rifle cartridges, they make longer-range shooting possible.

The .41 magnum is nearly as potent as the .44 and recoils even less, which is why some deer hunters prefer this oddball cartridge. I can't comment on its deer-killing effectiveness because I've never used it.

The author handgunned his first deer with a .44 magnum Ruger Super Blackhawk—still an excellent choice in the deer woods.

A wide variety of excellent revolvers—like this double-action Dan Wesson with interchangeable barrels—are chambered for the popular .44 magnum cartridge.

Smith & Wesson was the first to offer double-action .44 magnum revolvers. Gun and cartridge remain a top choice for handgun hunters willing to limit their shooting to less than one hundred yards.

Deer have been taken with .357 magnums, but few experienced handgunners today are willing to rely on this marginal round in the deer woods. I can't recommend using a .357 on anything larger than coyotes, although it's a fine choice for yodel dogs and smaller game.

When it was introduced back in 1956, the .44 magnum was considered the world's most powerful handgun (remember Dirty Harry?)—but only briefly. The considerably more potent .454 Casull was developed the following year. The .454 Casull used a proprietary load then chambered exclusively for single-action Casull (now Freedom Arms) revolvers. While the .454 was and is a great hunting cartridge, it packs more punch (and kicks harder) than necessary for deer-sized game. The .454's limited acceptance and availability kept the .44 magnum at the top of the handgun hunting game for many years. Today, more and more

While legal, the .357 magnum is marginal in the deer woods. The .41 magnum delivers less recoil than the .44 magnum, but offers real deer-killing power.

hunters are using the .454 Casull, and several manufacturers now offer handguns in this chambering.

Before Freedom Arms first introduced its impressive .454 Casull revolver, I visited the company's Freedom, Wyoming plant to help test a few early prototypes. We tried to destroy one by loading as much Bullseye powder as the lengthened, beefed-up .45 Colt brass would hold. We later tried an extreme-pressure triplex load (containing three different kinds of powder) topped by a slightly oversized bullet. We tied the gun to a bench, then tripped the trigger by pulling on a long string from behind a sturdy barricade. After one test, we had to pound the cylinder from the frame with a mallet, but the gun remained intact. It's possible to blow up one of these sturdy guns if the bore is obstructed or if you use insanely hot handloads, but they'll handle pressures unsafe in almost any other revolver.

In expert hands, the .454 Casull is capable of killing any game.

While the .44 magnum produced more kick than lesser revolver rounds, the .454 took handgun recoil to a whole new level. Frankly, the .454 wasn't much fun to shoot. It kicked noticeably harder and sharper than any other revolver round then available. Until you learned to handle its recoil, the .454 was difficult to control.

Despite the fact that the .454 Casull is a handful, this hot-stepping round really delivers. Its 240-grain bullet at 1,900 feet per second (fps) creates nearly a foot-ton of muzzle energy. That's roughly twice the punch packed by a .44 magnum. Until recently, this was the hands-down choice for anyone who hankered to hunt really big game with a revolver.

Once a propriety cartridge, this potent handgun round is now factory loaded by Winchester, Hornady, and other ammo companies. In addition to Freedom Arms, Ruger, Taurus, Magnum Research, and other gunmakers are currently manufacturing revolvers in .454 Casull chambering. Thompson/Center offers its single-shot Encore pistol in a .454 Casull.

Soon after the .454 Casull was introduced, John Linebaugh shortened a .45–70 case and loaded it with 0.475-inch bullets weighing between 320 and 440 grains. The faster .454 Casull still delivers more foot-pounds of energy, but the big, heavy .475 Linebaugh slugs pack similar game-killing punch. Factory 240-grain .454 Casull loads leave the muzzle at a sizzling 1,900 fps, while massive 420-grain .475 Linebaugh bullets loaded by Buffalo Bore are 550 fps slower. As a result, the .454 churns up 1,920 foot-pounds of energy at the muzzle, while the .475 Linebaugh manages only 1,700. As for hunting effectiveness, either of these behemoths will do the job.

Freedom Arms now offers its Model 83 revolver in .475 Linebaugh chambering. Factory loads are available from the Buffalo Bore Ammunition Company (P.O. Box 78, Carmen, ID

83462) and Hornady. Buffalo Bore offerings include a 420-grain, flat-nosed, hard lead bullet loaded to 950 fps for game weighing up to 800 pounds and the same bullet at 1,350 fps for game that could weigh a ton. There's also a lighter 400-grain jacketed hollowpoint at 1,350 fps and a custom load throwing a massive 440-grain bullet at 1,350 fps. Hornady's .475 Linebaugh factory loads start a 400-grain XTP bullet at 1,300 fps.

The first time I fired a .475 Linebaugh Freedom Arms revolver I found the recoil intimidating. I concentrated more on hanging onto the gun than hitting the target. But in comparison, .454 Casull recoil felt sharper—a sharp rabbit punch versus a hard shove—and was even less pleasant.

Magnum Research began offering massively oversized revolvers in 1998. Some of these big single-action guns feature cylinders of eye-popping proportions that swallow rifle cartridges like the .45/70 and the considerably hotter .450 Marlin. Fired in Marlin lever rifles, the .450 Marlin churns up 3,420 foot-pounds at the muzzle with 350-grain factory loads. In the Magnum Research revolver's 10⅝-inch barrels, this load still delivers an impressive 2,420 foot-pounds of punch. Put in perspective, that's a full one-third more energy than the 1,813 foot-pounds a 300-grain .454 Casull factory load delivers. And it's nearly 2½ times as powerful as a 300-grain .44 magnum.

"Sturdy" doesn't begin to describe Magnum Research's big five-shot single-action revolver. The gun is manufactured to close tolerances and is exceptionally well made. The oversized Hogue grips distribute recoil over a greater surface area, but I found them too large for comfort. I'd prefer a smooth grip that would allow the gun to rotate upward in my hand.

This is a hunting gun, pure and simple. No one is going to use the .450 Marlin BFR to shoot at targets or plink cans. At most

The Freedom Arms single-action revolver in .475 Linebaugh chambering is a potent weapon. Like the .454, it can be used to hunt anything.

This long-chambered five-shot single-action Magnum Research BFR revolver digests the potent .450 Marlin rifle cartridge.

hunting ranges, you'll need to use a rest like Stoney Point's Steady-Stix bipod.

I found its accuracy to be excellent. Three-shot groups at fifty yards averaged just one and half inches between centers. When testing handguns, I normally fire five-round groups, but after three consecutive shots my hands stung so badly I wasn't sure where the next round would go. I needed a five-minute break before repeating the exercise.

Yes, this big magnum kicks. As do the .454 Casull, the .475 Linebaugh, and Smith & Wesson's new .500 powerhouse. The .500 S&W magnum churns up more than 2,600 foot-pounds of energy, and it's the ultimate big-game stopper. The company introduced this monster in 2003, and had to build a new, massive X-frame revolver to handle the potent cartridge. Thanks to its built-in recoil compensator, Hogue-designed Sorbathane grips, and seventy-two-ounce heft, the Smith & Wesson Model 500 is no more painful to shoot than some smaller-caliber magnums. I should note, however, that this is only the case when the .500 S&W throws 275- or 325-grain bullets. When loaded hot with 400-grain or heavier projectiles, recoil is intimidating.

For real game-killing ability, revolvers offer the smashing punch of a .480 Ruger, .445 SuperMag, .450 Hornady, .454 Casull, or .475 Linebaugh. These guns aren't for everyone, but if you need a serious hunting handgun for tackling big game, all of these revolvers are up to the job.

The cartridges named above are available in double-action revolvers from Ruger, Dan Wesson, Smith & Wesson, Taurus, and other manufacturers, as well as in the excellent single-action sixguns made by Freedom Arms, Ruger, and Magnum Research.

While the above rounds are potent enough for any game on the continent—delivering more power than the average deer

Padded gloves help tame magnum recoil.

The title of "World's Most Powerful Revolver" is now held by the double-action .500 Smith & Wesson. This is the ultimate big-game stopper.

hunters wants or needs—their increased recoil definitely exacts a toll. I've fired all these super-magnum loads, but none are much fun to shoot after the first few rounds (although the .45–70 was a pussycat). They call for padded gloves and any other help you can find. Whenever I've fired any of these bigbore behemoths, practice sessions have been short and far between.

Heavy recoil is something serious big-game handgunners simply must learn to manage. With practice, you'll eventually be able to wring acceptable hunting accuracy from any of the big magnums. From a sandbagged rest at twenty-five yards, my Freedom Arms .475 Linebaugh punches highly satisfying 1¼-inch, five-shot groups when fed with relatively mild 420-grain loads at 950 fps. With hotter, harder-kicking fodder intended for really big game, my groups expand to 3½ inches or more. The longer I continue firing, the larger the groups.

SMALLBORE CENTERFIRE REVOLVERS

Not all hunting revolvers digest hard-kicking bigbore magnum rounds. I know of at least two wheelguns that chamber .22 Hornet centerfire loads. The .22 Hornet is a mild, soft-spoken cartridge suitable only for squirrels, prairie dogs, and similarly diminutive game.

When Taurus introduced the Raging Bull several years ago, it was first offered in .44 magnum, then .454 Casull and .480 Ruger chamberings. The Raging Bull is a big, burly handgun with a massive full-length shroud and distinctive ventilated rib. Barrels are available in 5-, 6½-, and 8⅜-inch lengths. These big-game hunting handguns weigh between fifty-one and sixty-three ounces.

Though built around the same bigbore Raging Bull frame, the Raging Hornet is even bigger, bulkier, and heavier. Drilling .22-caliber holes in the massive barrel and cylinder removes less steel than holes twice that diameter. The long ten-inch barrel adds to the heft, resulting in a 16½-inch handgun that tips the scales at an impressive eighty-four ounces. The gun has an eight-round capacity.

Supported by sandbags or a Steady-Stix bipod, the big revolver provides a remarkably steady platform. This double-deuce centerfire is designed for killing prairie dogs and ground squirrels at well beyond .22 rimfire range. Soon after the Raging Hornet was introduced, I had the chance to try it out during one of Chuck "The Dogfather" Cornett's annual Prairie Dog Conferences.

Before heading for the prairie dog towns, I chronographed 45-grain Winchester factory loads in the Raging Hornet. They averaged 1,890 fps. That's some 700 fps slower than you'd get from a .22 Hornet rifle, but it's still impressive zip from a handgun. To put things in perspective, that's roughly the same muzzle velocity that a .22 rimfire magnum rifle churns up when firing 40-grain loads. That put the Raging Hornet's effective range at somewhere between 100 and 150 yards.

The .22 Hornet revolver delivered very good accuracy. Using the gun's excellent Patridge-style adjustable sights and a

The Taurus Raging Hornet digests diminutive .22 Hornet rifle rounds.

sandbagged rest, I was able to fire 1⅛-inch, five-shot groups at fifty yards. In deference to my aging eyes, I installed the heavy-duty scope mount that was supplied with the gun. This attaches to the barrel via three small steel rectangles that are inserted through the slots in the rib, and then mated to the mount with a half-dozen hex-head screws. The mount features a series of Picatinny-style slots that accept Weaver rings.

I used the mount to install a Bushnell Holosight for the hunt. A long-eye-relief scope would be a better choice for hand-gunning over two hundred yards, but the Holosight is much faster and easier to use at closer .22 Hornet ranges.

Magnum Research also offers a .22 Hornet revolver. Unlike the extended-cylinder "Maxine" version of the company's big single-action gun, the "Little Max" wears a normal-sized cylinder made to digest .45 Colt, .454 Casull, and .50 A.E. cartridges—as well as the powder-puff .22 Hornet.

Taurus and Magnum Research faced real challenges when they decided to chamber revolvers for the .22 Hornet. Several years earlier, Smith & Wesson introduced the Model 53, a wheelgun chambered for the .22 Remington Jet, while Ruger trotted out the single-action Hawkeye, a single-shot pistol built on the Blackhawk revolver frame. This gun was designed specifically for .256 Winchester Magnum ammo. Both guns experienced problems with the bottlenecked cartridges they fired, and have long since disappeared from the scene. In contrast, the .22 Hornet Taurus and Magnum Research revolvers function flawlessly.

Fired in Magnum Research's Little Max revolver, factory 45-grain .22 Hornet loads exit the muzzle at 1,900 fps. That's 700 fps slower than a .22 Hornet rifle produces, but still an impressive speed from a sixgun. The .22 Hornet cylinder holds six rounds.

SINGLE-SHOT AND BOLT-ACTION PISTOLS

When the Thompson/Center Contender first appeared in 1967, the single-shot pistol featured easily interchangeable barrels. Cartridge choices ranged from .22 rimfire to centerfire rifle rounds like the .223, .30–30, and .45–70. The Contender was the first handgun to deliver rifle-like range and accuracy.

The Contender action wasn't strong enough to digest pressures generated by high-intensity rounds like the .243 and .308, so Thompson/Center later designed the Encore. Resembling a Contender on steroids, this sturdy pistol appeared in 1996. Like the Contender, the Encore allows several different barrels to be mounted on a single frame. But because the Encore was built specifically to handle loads the Contender can't safely digest, barrels aren't interchanged between the two models.

At last look, the Encore was offered in a whole slew of rifle chamberings, including .223, .22–250, .243, .25–06, .270, 7mm-

The Thompson/Center Encore is stronger than the company's Contender model, and will digest high-pressure rifle rounds.

08, .308, .30–06, .45–70, and .450 Marlin. Barrels are also available to handle handgun rounds like the .44 magnum, .45 Colt, .454 Casull, and .480 Ruger.

Hornady says the new .480 Ruger load generates only half the felt recoil of the .454 Casull. And after firing the .480 in an Encore, I'm inclined to agree. Compared to the .454, the .480 Encore is a pussycat to control.

Switching Encore or Contender barrels is easy. Simply unscrew the forearm, tap out the hinge pin, and remove the barrel from the frame. Install the replacement barrel in reverse order. Like the Contender, the Encore action is opened by simply pulling back on the trigger guard extension. Unlock the action and the barrel tips up under its own weight, exposing the chamber for easy loading. Unlike the old Contender, the Encore action doesn't need to be opened, then closed, before you can thumb the hammer back to the full-cock position. The redesigned G2 Contender offers this same convenience.

Thompson/Center pistols customized by SSK Industries (owned by handgunning pioneer J. D. Jones) are available chambered for a variety of hot-stepping wildcats designed for these sturdy single shots. These cartridges range from the .226 JDJ (J. D. Jones) through the big, booming .475 JDJ, which throws a 500-grain Barnes bullet at more than 1,500 fps. Energy with this particular load is an impressive 2,670 foot-pounds.

Because there's no gap between barrel and chamber (as in a revolver), expanding gases can't leak to the side before the bullet leaves the muzzle. As a result, fixed-breech pistols like T/C's Encore and Contender and Savage's bolt-action Striker produce higher velocities (and greater punch) than you get in a revolver.

When Savage unveiled the Striker in 1998, the pistol was built around a modified version of the time-proven Model 110 rifle action. Modifications included using a left-handed bolt to allow right-handed shooters to operate the action without removing their shooting hand from the grip.

The Striker is currently offered in calibers ranging from the .22 Long Rifle and .17 HMR rimfires to the .300 Winchester Short Magnum (WSM). The magazine of the .300 WSM Striker holds but a single, fat magnum round, giving the pistol a two-shot capacity. Non-magnum Strikers in .243, 7mm-08, and .308 chamberings accommodate a pair of loads in the blind magazine.

When I tested different .300 WSM loads in the Striker, the 180-grain Fail Safe bullet clocked 2,460 fps, while the 150-grain Ballistic Silvertip moved out at 2,704 fps. That's 500 and 600 fps less velocity than you'd expect from a rifle firing the same fodder.

Firing .300 WSM rounds in a 5½-pound pistol usually produces pretty stout recoil, but the well-designed, ambidextrous pistol grip made the gun surprisingly controllable. Rotating the innovative Savage Adjustable Muzzle Brake to the "on" position tamed recoil

J. D. Jones has taken a wide variety of game with the customized JDJ hand cannons he produces. Photo courtesy of J. D. Jones.

The Savage Striker is a bolt-action repeater chambered for rifle cartridges.

even further. Like all muzzle brakes, this one is very loud when engaged. You wouldn't want to fire the Striker without wearing ear protection anyway, but good earplugs or muffs are absolutely mandatory when the muzzle brake is operating. Rotating the brake to the "off" position significantly reduces muzzle blast, but sharply boosts recoil.

Remington and Weatherby once fielded bolt-action pistols chambered for high-velocity rifle rounds, but these guns are no longer in production. The Lone Eagle single shot from Magnum Research is another handgun capable of taking a wide variety of game. This rotating-breech pistol—once offered in fifteen chamberings ranging from the .22 Hornet to .358 Winchester—has also been recently discontinued.

AUTO PISTOLS

Auto pistols, like the popular .45 ACP Model 1911 and the 9mm Beretta U.S. military forces are now using, were designed

The one auto pistol that qualifies as a serious hunting gun is the massive Mark XIX from Magnum Research. It chambers cartridges ranging from the .357 magnum to the big .50 Action Express.

as personal defense or law enforcement weapons. The 9mm and .45 ACP ammo these and many other auto pistols digest aren't widely suitable for hunting large game. I have a Holosight-mounted Kimber 1911 that I sometimes harass prairie dogs with at one hundred yards, but no one would call this serious hunting. I've had fun showering dirt on a lot of prairie poodles, but my kill ratio with the big .45 is pretty dismal. Pistols chambered for 10mm cartridges are slightly more potent, but don't equal the striking power of the .44 magnum.

The one auto pistol that qualifies as a serious hunting handgun is the massive Mark XIX offered by Magnum Research. "Massive" is not an exaggeration. These big, burly autoloaders are available in your choice of six- or ten-inch barrels and weigh between 4½ and 5 pounds. They're chambered for a variety of cartridges ranging from the .357 magnum to the .50 Action Express.

Chapter 5

HANDGUN SIGHTS

Most handgun owners are familiar with the sights their guns came equipped with—and know how to use them. But while open sights are basic equipment, hunters often opt to install one of several different aftermarket sights. This may include replacing factory irons with upgraded open sights that offer more convenient and precise windage and elevation adjustments or perhaps are simply easier to see and use under typical hunting conditions.

Electronic red-dot sights and Bushnell's holographic-reticle Holosights are increasingly popular with hunting handgunners. When you look through these non-magnifying sights, you see a red or bright orange dot centered in the field of view. Simply dab this dot on the target and pull the trigger. Red-dot sights are extremely fast and easy to use, which makes them ideal for hunting.

For shooting at extended distance (anything much greater than fifty yards), handgun scopes are the answer. These specialized scopes are available in various magnifications and are "must-have" accessories for long-range handgunning.

Let's begin with the basics. To shoot any firearm accurately, some kind of sighting equipment is needed. Without sights, a handgunner with natural pointing instincts may hit a wastebasket-sized target at ten or fifteen yards, but greater precision is unlikely, particularly at long range. And when you hunt with a handgun, precise bullet placement is vital.

Bushnell's non-magnifying, holographic-reticle Holosight is becoming increasingly popular with hunting handgunners.

Simply superimpose the glowing reticle over the target and pull the trigger.

A century ago, handgunners had little choice in the sights they used. Most revolvers and auto pistols wore simple fixed sights. If the sights weren't "on" at a certain range or with a particular load, shooters compensated by using "Kentucky windage," meaning that if the bullet struck low and to the left, the handgunner simply aimed high and right of the target.

Today, nearly all handguns come from the factory equipped with open iron sights. This basic sighting equipment consists of two separate elements: a front sight projecting upward near the muzzle and a square-notched rear sight usually positioned at the rear of the receiver. In the days of Sam Colt, the rear sight was usually a narrow slot milled into the revolver's top strap. The front sight was a simple rounded blade. These revolvers were typically sighted in with a particular load before leaving the factory.

Theoretically, a new revolver would deliver its bullet to point of aim at a range of fifteen or twenty-five yards. Different ammo fired at other distances required some kind of adjustment to hit the

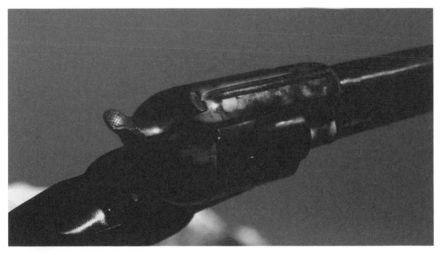

Single-action sixguns designed by Sam Colt sported a rear sight consisting of a narrow slot milled into the revolver's top strap.

mark. The rear sight was "fixed," so the most popular way to fine-tune accuracy was to bend the front sight to either side (for windage changes) and build it up or file it down to change elevation. Otherwise, a new front sight could be installed.

Similar rudimentary sights still exist on certain pistols and revolvers designed for concealed carry and personal defense. Because they lack sharp edges or protrusions, such sights are extremely rugged and won't hang up as the gun is drawn from a pocket or holster. Military handguns are usually issued with fixed sights because they're so rugged and virtually can't get out of adjustment. Fixed sights are favored when a fast, unhampered draw is desired and precise long-range marksmanship isn't a consideration. Most self-defense situations occur at seven yards or less, so pinpoint accuracy isn't required.

Some rear sights have only windage adjustments; changes in elevation must be made by filing down or increasing the height of the front sight blade. However, nearly all revolvers and most pistols designed for hunting are equipped with a moveable rear sight featuring micro-adjustments for windage (horizontal) and elevation (vertical) movements.

TAKING AIM

To aim an open-sighted handgun, look through the shallow notch in the rear sight and center the front blade in it. The top of the front blade should be level with the shoulders of the rear sighting notch to present an almost unbroken, continuous horizontal line. Retaining this front-sight, rear-sight relationship, move the gun until the target appears to rest atop the front sight blade. This is called the "six o'clock hold" (the front sight appears immediately below the target in the six o'clock position).

Throughout the firing process, the top of the front sight should remain level with the top of the rear sight. The same amount of daylight should appear on either side of the front sight to assure centering on target. The bull's-eye (or the portion of the animal you're aiming at) should appear to rest on top of the front sight.

Because front and rear sights are relatively close together on a handgun—and the gun itself is typically held at arm's length—young eyes may be able to keep both front and rear sight in fairly sharp focus. However, if you succeed in this, the target itself won't be in clear focus. It's impossible to keep all elements of the sight picture sharply focused. Concentrate too hard on the sights, and the target will blur around the edges. This is fine for target shooting, but it isn't a good idea in the hunting field.

When hunting with iron sights, I quickly verify that the front and rear sights are in proper alignment. Maintaining this relationship through peripheral vision, I focus on the front sight and the part of the animal at which it's pointed. Again, I use the six o'clock hold. The gun is sighted in to place the bullet exactly where the top of the front sight intersects the animal. This works only at a specific range. If the game is closer or farther away, you must adjust your aim accordingly. When firing at paper targets, I concentrate on the sights and let the bull's-eye blur. But when I aim at game, I focus on the front sight and target, and let the rear sight go fuzzy.

For precise long-range work, open sights are too coarse. At distances beyond forty or fifty yards, the front sight of a handgun looks wide enough to partially cover the bottom half of an animal. As the range increases, the more difficult pinpoint aiming becomes.

A handgun's front and rear sights are relatively close together, allowing shooters to keep both in fairly sharp focus. The longer the distance between these sights, the tougher it is to accomplish this.

Open iron sights are the most difficult handgun sights to use. Mastering them requires skill and practice. But isn't mastering challenges what handgun hunting is all about?

Of the various iron handgun sights on the market, target-style Patridge sights rank among the best. The Patridge sight features square-faced, sharply defined sighting surfaces. The rear sighting notch is relatively deep, with squared edges. When the front sight blade is properly centered in the notch, it's outlined by a thin strip of daylight on both sides.

Because Patridge-style sights were designed for target use, most are fully adjustable for elevation and windage. This allows the shooter to adjust the sights as he varies range and ammunition. Different loads and bullet weights tend to shoot to a different point of aim, so the ability to quickly change sight settings is important.

Some guns aren't properly sighted in when they leave the factory. Correcting this is easier if the gun wears adjustable sights. However, beware of precisely adjustable sights lacking in ruggedness. Hunting handguns are inevitably subject to a certain amount of abuse, such as exposure to dust, rain, or snow or the jouncing vibration of a hunting vehicle on rural roads. Fragile components have a way of failing in wilderness country where spares aren't readily available. Handgun hunters seldom change sight settings in the field, so adjustments are rarely needed.

As already noted, some guns are equipped with simple, non-adjustable fixed sights. Changes in elevation are made by filing down the front sight to raise the point of impact on target or increasing the height of the front sight to lower the bullet strike. The latter may also be accomplished by filing down the top of the rear sight. Some fixed sights are attached to the gun via a notch machined into the top strap or slide. These dovetail-mounted sights can be drifted sideways for rough changes in windage.

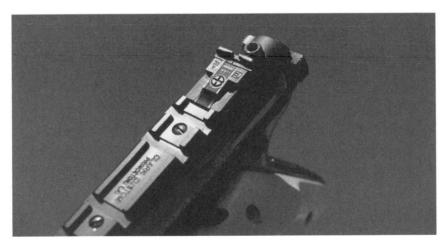

Hunters who use open-sighted handguns need a rear sight that is fully adjustable for windage and elevation.

Remember, when working with adjustable sights, move the rear sight in the same direction you want the point of impact on target to move. If the bullets are striking low and to the left of the aiming point, move the rear sight up and to the right. Since front and rear sights are viewed in opposition to each other, moving the front sight to the right has the same effect as adjusting the rear sight to the left.

Adjustable sights usually have click-stop increments built into the adjusting mechanism. Each click of the adjusting screw moves point of impact a certain distance. If your handgun sights are calibrated for one-inch increments at twenty-five yards, each "detent" (click) of the adjusting screw moves the bullet strike an inch at twenty-five yards, two inches at fifty yards, three inches at seventy-five yards, and so on.

Iron sights have the advantage of being fairly fast and easy to use, and add little or no bulk to the gun. Most holsters are designed for this kind of standard sighting equipment, and some kinds of target competition allow no other variety.

HANDGUN SCOPES

For handgunners who want to shoot game at longer distances, magnifying scope sights are the answer. Telescopic sights were once the exclusive province of riflemen, but specialized scopes specifically designed for handguns are now widely available. One major difference between rifle and handgun scopes is that rifle scopes are held within three or four inches of the shooter's eye, while handgun scopes are used at arm's length. Scopes designed for handguns are said to have long eye relief (usually from ten to twenty inches).

Another difference is that most handgun scopes offer relatively low magnification. Since a rifle is supported by a shoulder stock, as well as both hands, it's a more stable shooting platform. This makes relatively high magnification useful. The most practical magnification for a handgun scope may be 1 1/2X or 2X. Low-powered pistol scopes are popular, although some models offer 4X, 5X, or even 12X magnification. Handgun scopes are available in fixed or variable power.

But it's difficult to hold a handgun steady enough to take advantage of much more than 2X magnification. Long-range varmint shooters who mount high-X scopes on their handguns invariably shoot from sandbags, a bipod, or some other supportive rest.

Since the aiming crosshairs appear in the same visual plane as the target, both reticle (crosshairs) and target can be seen in sharp focus. Also, narrow crosshairs make very precise marksmanship possible.

Burris, Bushnell, Leupold, Nikon, Sightron, Thompson/ Center, and Nikon offer a variety of long-eye-relief scopes designed specifically for handgun use. Several different mounting systems are also available, some of which require no gunsmithing or alteration of the firearm during installation.

Ruger's Redhawk .44 magnum revolver was the first production handgun to be offered complete with integral scope mount and rings, giving the gunner a handy choice between open iron factory sights and a magnifying pistol scope. A scope can be mounted in seconds by simply turning a pair of screws. The screws activate a set of clamps that fit mating slots dovetailed into the barrel rib. Loosening these screws allows the scope to be dismounted immediately so the Redhawk's open iron sights can be used. Other scope mounts are available that allow similar quick-detach versatility on certain handguns.

While magnifying handgun sights make long-distance accuracy possible, they have some definite disadvantages. In the first

For handgunners who want to shoot longer distances, magnifying scope sights are the answer. Long-eye-relief means these scopes must be held ten to twenty inches from the shooter's eye.

place, adding a scope sight to any handgun greatly increases gun weight and bulk. The result is often a piece of shooting equipment that is badly balanced, one that must be carried by hand or in a custom or semi-custom holster rig designed specifically for scoped handguns.

Another huge downside is the tiny, relatively dim viewing field. This problem becomes progressively greater with increased magnification. Because even a 1 1/2X handgun scope offers a limited field of view, it takes longer to find the target in the reticle. (Powerful 10X or 12X handgun scopes are mostly practical for shooting prairie dogs.) Also, your eye must be directly behind the eyepiece before the target is visible in the scope. Because precise eye-to-scope alignment is more difficult when the gun is held at arm's length, handgun scopes are harder to use.

Parallax is yet another problem with handgun scopes. This is the displacement of the reticle or crosshairs in relation to the target as the shooter's head moves to either side when aiming. A

Long-range pistols like this Thompson/Center G2 Contender usually mount handgun scopes.

rifleman's head is more or less held in position by the butt-stock, which mini-mizes parallax prob-lems. Handgunners have no such sup-port. Excessive par-allax can cause a bullet to miss its target, even though the sights may ap-pear to be in proper alignment. Again, this problem is greater as magnifi-cation increases.

ELECTRONIC (RED-DOT) SIGHTS

Several years ago, the Swedish company Aimpoint introduced a practical alternative to iron or scope sights. This non-magnifying electronic sight shows a bright orange dot projected over the target as you look through the reticle. You can view the target with both eyes open, making this sight extremely fast to use. Parallax isn't a problem, as both reticle (orange dot) and target appear in the same visual plane. Hunters and plinkers alike have used the Aimpoint and other dot-projecting sights on handguns with good

Electronic red-dot sights are fast and easy to use.

success, and many serious target competitors swear by the battery-powered sight.

Bushnell's Holosight works on the same principle used in the heads-up holographic displays that help F-14 fighter pilots instantly get on target. A laser-illuminated reticle appears as a holograph that seems to float at the target plane. Eye alignment isn't critical. Simply superimpose the reticle—a bright orange dot surrounded by an orange circle—on the target, and the shot goes where you want it. Reticle intensity can be easily varied. Again, no magnification means that you can use the Holosight with both eyes open. That gives you a virtually unlimited field of view and makes sighting extremely fast.

The Burris SpeedDot 135 operates in pretty much the same way as Aimpoint sights. Either 3 MOA (minute of angle) or 11 MOA aiming dots are available. Reticle brightness is continually variable through 11 click-stop settings.

Red-dot sights are popular for plinking, hunting, and target shooting.

At last look, red-dot handgun sights were available from Aimpoint, Burris, Bushnell, BSA, C-More, Millett, Nikon, Sightron, Tasco, Trijicon, and Ultra Dot.

One disadvantage of using battery-powered electronic sights on a hunting handgun is the possibility of failure in rough country. While some of these sights are highly reliable, they can't match the ruggedness of good iron sights. Today's handgun scopes also have a good reputation for reliability afield.

Chapter 6

HUNTING SMALL GAME WITH RIMFIRES

I shot my first jackrabbit when I was eight years old, wandering my grandfather's farm with his single-shot Winchester .22. A few years later I hunted rabbits and other game with a .22 rifle of my own. When I was seventeen and finally allowed to own a handgun, I ordered a French-made .22 auto pistol from Montgomery Ward. In those days, you could legally buy mail-order handguns, and Montgomery Ward offered time payments—a real boon to a struggling teenager with a nonexistent budget.

That first autoloader was neither reliable nor very accurate. Jamming was a frequent problem, and the fixed sights it wore were hard to see and shot high and to the right. But I loved that handgun. I hunted rabbits with it every chance I got. It was nowhere near as sure as the .22 rifle I owned, but hunting with a handgun seemed a lot more fun.

Later on, I acquired several other .22 handguns. The list included a couple of budget-priced Harrington & Richardson revolvers, a single-action Colt Frontier Scout, and Ruger and Smith & Wesson revolvers. I killed jackrabbits, ground squirrels, and tree squirrels with each and every one. Other critters that fell to carefully aimed Long Rifle bullets included a rattlesnake I almost stepped on when hunting rabbits, a bad-tempered badger that tried facing me down, and a handful of chicken coop–raiding skunks. Somewhere along the way, I learned how to shoot a handgun safely and with reasonable accuracy. I also developed a love of handgun hunting.

Every handgunner needs at least one .22 pistol or revolver. Rimfire guns shoot low-cost, low-recoil .22-caliber ammunition that can't be reloaded. Centerfire handguns are much more powerful, usually shoot bullets of larger caliber (diameter), and use more costly ammunition.

Even if you plan to hunt deer or other large game with a handgun, you should learn gun-handling basics with a .22 rimfire before graduating to larger, more powerful centerfire guns. If

Every handgunner needs at least one .22 pistol or revolver. Ammo is inexpensive, and recoil virtually nonexistent.

you intend to hunt only rabbits or squirrel-sized game, you may never need anything larger than a rimfire .22. For the beginner, casual plinker, or expert, at least one rimfire is a must in the handgun battery. And if you own just one handgun, it should probably be a .22.

Why? In the first place, .22 rimfire handguns are fun to shoot. Most rimfire handguns are quiet enough to let you shoot without flinching. Just don't neglect to use proper ear protection. Surprisingly, .22s are more likely to cause permanent ear damage than considerably louder, hard-kicking magnum centerfires. Rimfires are sneaky. Because .22s (even short-barreled handguns) aren't unpleasantly loud, too many shooters don't bother wearing earplugs or muff-type protectors. This is a big mistake. Even .22 Long Rifle rounds generate enough decibels to damage fragile cilia in the ear canal. Eventually this causes irreversible, permanent hearing damage.

The recoil these guns produce is almost nonexistent, and after the first shot or two the rankest beginner should be shooting them comfortably. Equally important is the fact that .22 rimfire ammo is cheap enough that you can shoot to your heart's content. Stepping up to a .22 WMR (Winchester Magnum Rimfire) or hot .17 HMR (Hornady Magnum Rimfire) adds some expense, but these loads are still affordable.

Stoking a .357 magnum or Colt .45 gets expensive fast—and unless you save those empty cartridge cases and reload them yourself, an afternoon of handgunning can be prohibitively costly. On the other hand, it's almost impossible to shoot up enough .22 fodder to dent the budget too badly in a single day.

Centerfire handguns—particularly those chambered for magnum or bigbore hunting cartridges—are very loud and generate heavy recoil. Learning to shoot a handgun is difficult enough without all that fuss and noise. More than a few first-time shooters give up after firing half a dozen rounds through their brand-new booming magnums.

Even if recoil and muzzle blast don't discourage you, the fact that you can't hit anything soon will. Simply firing a handgun is a far cry from hitting a distant target. And while some adults seem happy merely making loud bangs, most shooters become discouraged if that barrage of bullets fails to find the mark — or at least come reasonably close.

It's possible to learn to shoot with a centerfire handgun, but that's doing it the hard way. Beginning handgunners are much

better off learning the basics with a .22 rimfire.

Once the basics of gun handling, trigger control, safety, stance, and sight picture are learned, the shooter can move up to the centerfires. As a matter of fact, shooting the .22 can prove so much fun and so rewarding you may

The Smith & Wesson .22 rimfire shown at right is a near twin to the .44 magnum revolver the company also offers. Initial shooting skills are best learned with a .22.

never feel the need for a more powerful handgun. For plinking and informal target shooting, the .22 is your number-one choice. The rimfire is also adequate for taking small game. It's the one handgun the entire family can enjoy shooting.

Even if you graduate to the potent centerfire cartridges required for hunting deer or larger game, you'll never outgrow that soft-spoken .22.

CHOOSING A RIMFIRE HANDGUN

The .22 rimfire chambering is available in a wide variety of revolvers, auto pistols, and single-shot handguns.

Among the rimfire autoloaders on the market, the Ruger Mark II stands out as a top value. Available in target and standard models, it offers proven reliability and exceptional quality—along with a very affordable price. The target model features fully adjustable target sights and slightly greater heft. The standard model costs a bit less, and is also a fine-shooting handgun. If you can afford the higher price tag, the Mark II Target gun is easier to steady on target and shoot accurately. I've hunted with a Mark II target model for several years, and recently had it customized by pistolsmith Dino Longueira.

There are many other .22 auto pistols on the market. These range from short-barreled pocket pistols not really suitable for hunting to very high-priced target guns used in serious competition. Browning, Smith & Wesson, SIG Arms, and other gunmakers offer good rimfire self-loaders at reasonable prices.

There's a good variety of .22 revolvers on the market, and most are capable of solid hunting performance. Rimfire revolvers offer the advantage of digesting all three lengths of popular .22 cartridges—short, long, and Long Rifle—interchangeably. Most auto pistols will function properly only when .22 Long Rifle ammo is used, although some target pistols fire .22 shorts exclusively.

Ruger's Mark II auto pistol is a favorite of rabbit hunters.

The Browning BuckMark is a popular plinking and hunting .22 auto pistol.

Smith & Wesson, Ruger, and Dan Wesson offer fine .22 revolvers suitable for plinking and precision target use. Smith & Wesson's .22 Kit Gun is a favorite of outdoorsmen, while Ruger's double-action rimfires remain in high demand. Dan Wesson makes a .22 revolver with interchangeable barrels, so you can vary the configuration of your gun. These double-action revolvers are extremely accurate and can be had in either blued steel or stainless steel.

Sturm, Ruger & Company offers a totally modern single-action .22 sixgun, although its "plowhandle" design does evoke a certain amount of nostalgia. The Ruger rimfire is a sturdy, totally reliable gun offered in blued or stainless steel. The Freedom Arms single-action .22 is another top-quality revolver that will give several lifetimes of service.

Plinking with a S&W .22 revolver will develop the skills necessary to shoot well with a S&W centerfire like the one on the author's hip.

The Thompson/Center Contender break-top single shot is offered in .22 rimfire chambering and makes a very accurate, if slow-firing, handgun.

There are a number of .22 "novelty" guns available, including tiny derringers that do double duty as belt-buckle decorations. These Lilliputian handguns are of little use to sportsmen.

Even with .22 rimfires, quality can vary widely, as can price. Generally speaking, the old adage of "getting what you pay for" applies. Always buy the best quality you can afford when purchasing a new handgun. An inexpensive .22 can provide a lot of low-cost pleasure, but a better-made model will provide even more fun for a much longer time.

Rimfires are versatile. Lynn Thompson shot these spring hares, rabbits, and porcupines with his .22 magnum Model 252 Freedom Arms revolver. Photo courtesy of Lynn Thompson.

PISTOLERO STEAKAGE

You don't necessarily need a rimfire handgun to hunt small, edible game. Rock legend Ted Nugent knows that any handgun you have handy will do the job. Here, Nugent shares his thoughts on handgunning for small game.

If guns cause crime, all of mine are defective. And if handguns are made only for killing people, as the actions of Sarah Brady and her friends like Dianne Feinstein and Charlie Schumer would suggest, then swimming pools are made only for drowning and ladders only for falling off. Sheer, unadulterated nonsense.

The percentage of murders committed with handguns is such an infinitesimal number as to be laughable. It is negligent to somehow blame the 99.999 percent of good guys for the illegal misuse by the handful of mostly paroled dirt. Remember, the actual numbers from government law enforcement, safety, health, and medical agencies report that larger percentages of injuries and deaths occur from accidents involving ladders and swimming holes than all firearms combined, much less just handguns. We won't even look at the carnage from automobiles, electricity, and farm machinery. Bottom line: Handguns and law-abiding handgunners are cool.

Now that we have put the dishonest propaganda to rest, let us celebrate the true fact that millions upon millions of law-abiding firearms enthusiasts all across America enjoy a multitude of recreational, Olympic, self-defense, law enforcement, competitive, and sporting use of handguns each and every day of the year. Millions. Every day. And according to the National Safety Council, fewer firearm-related injuries and accidents occur per one hundred thousand usages than those involving boating, skiing, golf, tennis, football, baseball, camping, and myriad other activities. The truth is, if you want to be safer, get a gun and carry it. Works for me.

I've been using .22 revolvers and semi-autos for small game for more than thirty years. Many a squirrel, rabbit, grouse, and other small game has been brought to the Nugent dinner table by handgun. Other actions in .22 magnum, .38 special, .38 super, .380, .45, .40, 9mm, 10mm, .44 special, .41, and .44 magnum have proven practical and effective for me, as well.

Some may guess that the larger, more powerful loads would be too much for smaller game, but even the .44 magnum doesn't destroy much meat on game like a rabbit because the bullet will normally plow clean through the critter, disrupting little and causing only slight tissue damage, but killing quickly and cleanly. Ya gotta love that. McNuggets should have it so good.

Rabbits are always popular quarry for rimfire handgunners.

Living on and managing wonderful Midwest American farm-ground most of my life, a readily accessible handgun has made a tremendous difference on the varmint population in our bailiwick. While rabies and distemper have reached epidemic proportions across much of the land, we have no such problem on Swamp Nuge. Why? Because both of those life-threatening maladies and others like them are a direct result of overpopulation among raccoons, skunks, possums, and an explosion of free-ranging feral dogs and cats. We have no such problem in our rural neighborhood, or at least on our property, because we always shoot and kill the surplus of these otherwise uncontrollable critters, thereby eliminating the indiscriminate diseased hand of Ma Nature.

Though many folks cringe at the thought of whacking cute little furbearers, that kind of uneducated ignorance is the very cause of rampant infestations of disease and even the death of innocent children. If kids dying of rabies is no concern of yours, you need help and your criticism is unfounded, immoral, counterproductive, and just plain foolish. I haven't the time. Shoot a raccoon, save a kid. It's that simple.

With a handgun at my side throughout my life, I have taken great pleasure in honing my proficiency with my choice of carry gun. While most of my wilderness strolls are with bow and arrows in hand, I gain great satisfaction in casual woodland strolls with only my sidearm accompanying my family and me.

I aim for pistolero steakage—from edible small game like rabbit to edible big game like . . . well, you name it.

I was walking back up my long marsh-surrounded driveway one cold winter morning with my five hounds, celebrating all things Spirit of the Wild. I had just fetched the Sunday paper and tucked it under my left arm when the dogs all flash-pointed a large brushpile. Gonzo, the big chocolate Lab, lunged into the thicket and a fat, furry cottontail rabbit erupted out the other side, rocketing away in the snow.

In an instant, with the zipper already halfway up on my long, insulated Ducks Unlimited parka, I yanked my Glock M20, 10mm from the form-fitting Galco hip holster and swung one-handed on the fleeing bunny.

At about thirty yards, just as the scrambling ball of fur was about to enter a beachball-sized hole in the puckerbrush, the handy, Mag-na-ported Glock went *bang* and the rabbit rolled head over heels into the snow. I never saw my sights, and it could well have been the very best instantaneous shot I have ever made with any weapon in my life. Sure, I'm bragging, cuz it was sensational—and after all, that's why I shoot all the time, so I can get good. Getting good at stuff is why we live, isn't it?

The real point, though, is that if a goofy old guitar player can do it, anybody can, including you. Honing handgun-eye coordination comes from constant—repeat, constant—step-by-step re-hearsals of the shooting procedure.

Shooting is always fun. Shooting *always* is even more fun. Buy ammo and shoot it up. You will be moved.

Hunting with rimfire handguns can easily be an end in it-self. All handguns present challenges rifles can't equal, and using a .22 pistol or revolver to put game on the table can be highly re-warding. And if rimfires begin to pale, hunting with centerfire handguns is only a short step away.

Chapter 7

PISTOLS AND PRAIRIE DOGS— LONG-RANGE VARMINT SHOOTING

Shoot prairie dogs with handguns? At three hundred yards or more? I used to think it was a silly idea—a stunt. I'd always used heavy-barreled rifles whenever I hunted varmints at long range. A good, properly scoped varmint rifle could be relied on to reach out and kill marmots, prairie dogs, and other pests at eye-boggling distances. With the help of a bipod or sandbagged rest, a steady-handed rifleman can hit Coke bottle–sized targets at 350 or 400 yards with monotonous regularity.

Then I made a surprising discovery. Bull-barreled varmint rifles weren't the only firearms suited for long-range prairie dogging. Some hybrid handguns mounting long-eye-relief scopes were capable of similar 300-plus-yard accuracy. When Thompson/Center introduced the single-shot Contender more than thirty years ago, it changed the entire concept of hunting with a

Thompson/Center's single-shot Encore and Contender pistols digest long-range rifle rounds and are accurate enough to kill prairie dogs at three hundred yards or more.

handgun. In addition to conventional handgun cartridges, the break-top Contender was also chambered for several different rifle cartridges. It was also the first production handgun with a handful of barrels that could be quickly and easily swapped.

You could hunt deer with a .30–30, .44 magnum, or .45–70 barrel, then switch to a .22 Hornet or .223 tube for shooting prairie dogs, marmots, and other hole-digging, grass-guzzling pests that ranchers hated.

The Contender did a lot to popularize long-eye-relief pistol scopes. It was one handgun that cried out for optical sights. It was easy to mount a scope, and the magnified image the scope provided made it surprisingly easy to hit nine-inch-tall prairie dogs at varmint-rifle ranges.

It took me a while to warm up to the idea, but when I finally gave it a try, "pistoling" prairie dogs was a lot more fun than I thought it would be. I'd taken a fair number of rabbits and squirrels with rimfire pistols and sixguns over the years, shooting them offhand at thirty or forty yards and missing as many as I hit. Later, I hunted desert jackrabbits with a Remington XP-100 shortly after this strange, bolt-action handgun and its .221 Fireball cartridge were first introduced. The mid-handled pistol was awkward to use, and by the time I'd found a steady shooting position the rabbit was usually long gone. Disenchanted, I forgot about handgun hunting and returned to my faithful, familiar rifles.

Then I became acquainted with the late Bob Milek, and hunted prairie dogs with him a couple of times. I used a rifle, while he relied on a customized Thompson/Center Contender. Watching him shoot, I was astonished at his long-range handgunning skills. He convinced me that even I could—with practice—kill picket pins with a scoped pistol at nearly the same distance as

In expert hands, scoped centerfire pistols make long-range rifle accuracy a real possibility.

my bull-barreled varmint rifle. With his encouragement, I acquired a scoped .223 Contender and included it in my varmint-shooting battery.

I always bring several firearms along when I head for prairie dog country, but in the last few years the mix has changed. I once packed two or three varmint rifles and a single scoped handgun in my traveling gun cases. Now I'm more likely to tote two or three pistols and a lone rifle to weekend varminting expeditions.

When I attended one of Chuck Cornett's annual prairie dog conferences in Montana, I brought a lightweight .223 Kimber varmint rifle and a pair of handguns with me. One was a .22–250 T/C Encore mounting a 2.5–7X T/C pistol scope. The Encore punched ¾-inch groups at one hundred yards with factory ammo and was great for extended-range shooting.

The other handgun was Taurus's newly introduced Raging Hornet. With iron sights, the .22 Hornet revolver delivered 1⅛-inch groups at fifty yards. Winchester 45-grain factory loads chronographed at 1,890 fps through the Hornet's ten-inch barrel. That's 700 fps slower than a .22 Hornet rifle delivers, or roughly the same *oomph* you get from a .22 WMR rifle firing 40-grain ammo. Those velocities pegged the Raging Hornet's effective range at 100 yards to a maximum of maybe 140 yards.

I planned using the revolver exclusively for close-in shots, so instead of attaching a long-eye-relief scope to the Taurus, I mounted a Bushnell Holosight. A 6X or 7X pistol scope delivers an agonizingly tiny field of view, making aiming painfully slow. The Holosight allowed me to find the target a lot faster and provided all the precision I needed out to one hundred yards. And mounting the Holosight promptly halved the size of the groups I'd been shooting.

I was paired with J. B. Hodgdon, of Hodgdon Powder fame. He alternated between a custom-stocked Remington XP-100 and a T/C Encore. We both used Stoney Point's Steady-Stix bipods to steady our handguns. It was a hot, cloudless day, and shots ranged from sixty yards out to nearly four hundred yards.

While it was too warm for comfort, shooting over a populous prairie dog town thankfully requires almost no walking and stalking. Once you find a good spot, you unload your bench and sandbags or get comfortable behind a bipod rest. When the shooting is good, you can spend most of the day in the same location. Prairie dog shooting is almost perfectly suited to long-range handgunning. You can take plenty of time setting up—and once your bipod, pistol, ammo, binoculars, and other gear are handily arranged, you can simply sit, spot, and shoot.

Another great thing about hunting prairie dogs is that you never worry about wounding one, even when the range is ridiculously long. Whether you're using a .22 centerfire pistol or a bull-barreled varmint rifle, chances are you'll either vaporize the critters or score a clean miss. Few prairie poodles shot by high-velocity centerfire handguns die a lingering death.

One important difference between long-range rifles and scoped handguns is that it's possible to fire a rifle from the unsupported standing, sitting, or kneeling positions and still hit prairie dogs at considerable distances. But don't even think about shooting a scoped pistol offhand at varmint-sized critters. Rifle scopes sport relatively short-eye-relief—usually three to five inches. To see through a pistol scope reticle, you must hold it ten to twenty inches in front of your eye. Even if your arms are strong enough to extend a five- to seven-pound scoped pistol at arm's length for more than a few seconds, it's impossible to hold it steady enough for accurate aiming. Whenever

J. B. Hodgdon takes aim at a distant prairie dog.

I've tried this, the barrel wobbles like a starving supermodel in a hurricane.

Attempting long-distance shooting from the kneeling or sitting position offers similar problems. Move a long-eye-relief scope far enough forward to see through the reticle and there's no support directly underneath the handgun. Shooting prairie dogs with a scoped pistol calls for a bipod or a sandbagged rest.

We had lots of action the first day of the hunt. There was little wind to speak of, and dozens of dogs basked happily on their mounds, oblivious to the sun's cancerous rays. Then again, cancer was the least of the problems they faced that day.

I spent the first hour or so shooting my Kimber rifle, killing prairie dogs between 250 and 400 yards downrange. Then I laid the rifle aside and used handguns the rest of the day. J. B. and I sat

The late Bob Milek with one of his favorite "prairie-dogging" pistols—a customized XP-100.

on the open prairie overlooking hundreds of mounds that stretched to the far horizon. J. B. was downright deadly. I spotted for him as he terminated a dozen prairie dogs, some at outlandish distances. It's hard to get accurate laser rangefinder readings in flat, open country, but I know a few of his kills were made at distances well beyond 400 yards.

With my aging eyes, I have a hard time even seeing these diminutive critters through a pistol scope at that kind of range. Still, I managed to kill a half-dozen picket pins standing on their burrows nearly that far away. It's a big help to have someone else watching the target through a binocular. A spotter can tell you if you hit or miss—and if it's a miss, how far above, below, or to one side the bullet kicked up dust. A bull-barreled .223 varmint rifle with a high-powered scope attached usually has enough recoil-dampening heft to allow you to see your own bullet strike, particularly with the scope set at 10X or less. But a handgun doesn't. It'll move off target every time, even with only a 4X or 6X scope.

J. B. Hodgdon supports his T/C Encore on Stoney Point's Steady-Stix bipod.

A sandbagged rest makes a rock-steady shooting position.

When long shots were involved J. B. and I took turns spotting and shooting. This wasn't necessary at ranges under two hundred yards, but gunning at longer distances often required repeated windage and elevation corrections before the bullet finally struck the target. That's another great thing about shooting prairie dogs—you can miss several times, and they'll usually hang around to give you second (or third or fourth) chance. Deer are rarely that accommodating—but prairie dogs make much tinier targets.

The shooting was steady, and we counted coup on a fair number of dogs before calling it a day.

When we set out early the next morning, the sun was already beating down hard. By eleven o'clock the temperature had soared to 102 degrees—too hot for many of the prairie dogs, that lounged comfortably underground in their cool, safe burrows. Shooting was a lot slower that day, but there was still enough action to keep us hopefully scanning the prairie. One dog surprised me by popping from a mound just eighty yards away.

This was a job for the Raging Hornet. I set aside my Encore and picked up the 16½-inch, 5¼-pound revolver. I hadn't done much shooting with the new gun before the hunt, and its action was still a little stiff. The single-action trigger broke crisply at 4½ pounds—a tad heavy, but not too bad.

The Taurus was sighted in at one hundred yards, so I simply centered the big, orange Holosight dot on the prairie dog's chest and squeezed the trigger. Even at that range, the .22 Hornet didn't kill as explosively as the hotter centerfires, but it still did the job very nicely. The fact that the critter remained mostly intact allowed me to take a few not-too-gory photos.

During the past several years, I've shot prairie dogs with a number of different long-range handguns. They included a rear-handled XP-100 from Remington's Custom Shop and an

The author poses with a prairie dog he shot with a Holosight-equipped Taurus Raging Hornet.

equally nice Weatherby Mark V CFP. Unfortunately, these fine, bolt-action pistols are no longer in production. I've also used Magnum Research's Lone Eagle single shot (also on the endangered list), as well as a couple of Savage Striker repeaters.

While it's not intended for long-range shooting, I've used a Holosight-mounted 1911 Kimber to worry prairie dogs at ranges up to one hundred yards. But this was simply a stunt. I've killed a few unlucky poodles with the big .45, but I've sprayed harmless dirt on many others. I planned on taking the Holosighted Kimber along on the last prairie dog shoot I attended, but organizers decreed that bullets heavier than 60 grains wouldn't be allowed.

While I missed the chance to work on my long-range .45 ACP marksmanship I could see some sense in the rule. In some cases, hunting parties would be positioned less than a mile apart. A fast-stepping .22 centerfire slug is likely to disintegrate on impact with anything it strikes. A 230-grain pistol slug loafing along at subsonic velocities is almost guaranteed to ricochet. Safety is the number-one concern of any handgun hunter.

Before I began handgunning varmints at extended range, I often used a scoped or Holosight-equipped rimfire pistol to shoot ground squirrels. The range was usually short enough that an open-sighted .22 could do the job. Prairie dogs are larger and considerably shier, but can also be killed with a well-aimed rimfire slug at distances closer than fifty yards. Beyond that range, 40-grain Long Rifle slugs lack the power to anchor the heavier prairie dogs.

I still shoot rifles at various kinds of varmints—but when prairie dogs are the target, I get extra enjoyment from using a scoped .22 centerfire handgun. Pistols like the Thompson/Center Encore or Contender, as well as the bolt-action Savage Striker, are capable of the same long-range accuracy that was once only possible with rifles. Striker varmint-rifle chamberings include the .22 WMR, .17 HMR, and .223.

An accurate handgun firing hot-stepping .22 centerfire loads will take prairie dogs at surprisingly long distances.

Anschutz, the German manufacturer of rimfire target-rifle fame, is also getting in on the act. It offers a neat little varmint pistol chambered for either .22 Hornet or .22 Long Rifle ammo. The Exemplar Hornet features an Anschutz Match 54 target rifle action, but—like the Savage Striker—it has the bolt handle moved to the left side so right-handed shooters needn't move their trigger hand from the stock. The bolt-action repeater wears a twenty-inch tube and tips the scales at an even five pounds.

So, should you hunt prairie dogs with pistols? Rifles may be easier to shoot, but I now find long-range handgunning even more exciting and rewarding.

Chapter 8

HANDGUNNING PREDATORS

The first time I tried calling coyotes into handgun range was almost my last. It was well past midnight as I sat nestled among some tall sagebrush, impatiently waiting for action. I was hunting Utah's west desert, only thirty-five miles from home — but starlight and shadows gave the familiar landscape an eerie, forbidding appearance. I might have been on Mars.

In my headlamp's feeble light, the desert glowed pale red, fading to blackness in just a few short yards. For the past five minutes my Circe call had been bleating an injured jackrabbit lament. I hoped it was convincing. With luck, I'd spot the red reflection of shining eyes as an animal came loping in.

I'd had good luck early and late in the day calling foxes and coyotes into easy rifle range. But because predators like the graveyard shift, this time I was calling late at night. I was missing some much-needed sleep, but I hoped the payoff would be a few prime yodel dog pelts.

While long accustomed to varmint rifles, this time I held a .223 Thompson/Center Contender with a 4X pistol scope attached. At arm's length, the long-eye-relief scope offered a constricted field of view that looked a lot dimmer at night. My red lamp provided little illumination, so I wouldn't get any long-range opportunities. My shots would have to be close.

I gave squalling a two-minute rest, and then began working the call again. Just seconds after I'd begun blasting away, my ears caught the sound of scrabbling claws. A moment later something heavy struck me full in the chest. Eager to beat the neighborhood coyotes to lunch, a hungry fox had blindly launched itself at the mouth-watering noise.

I don't know who was more startled. The fox and I "yiped" at the same time. Then we parted company.

I couldn't speak for the fox, but I was through for the night. Bed suddenly sounded awfully good—and I needed a fresh change of pants.

After too much excitement while calling at night, the author now sings to desert coyotes during daytime only.

Hunting varmints at night is always exciting—a fact that was reinforced a few months later when Del Mar Leach and I climbed partway up American Fork Canyon at 2:00 AM. The canyon was a noted bobcat hotspot, and we both wanted a kitty rug. Barring that, there was also an excellent chance of calling foxes or coyotes into handgun range.

I was carrying the same .223 T/C Contender, this time wearing a lower-powered 2X scope. I'd decided a wider field of view was the way to go. Del toted his favorite handgun—an iron-sighted .357 magnum single-action Ruger Blackhawk. According to a good friend who'd taken several bobcats in the vicinity, early—*early*—morning was the best time to call these wary critters, which much preferred dark to daylight.

Our headlamp lenses were covered with red cellophane, and we each had "rabbit-in-distress" calls in our pockets. The night was clear, with a cool touch of impending fall in the air. Perfect weather for calling.

We hiked several hundred yards up the mountainside, finally reaching the large clearing that was our destination. The clearing was loosely ringed by low trees and pockets of brush—great bobcat cover. Rocky cliffs towered above on either side. After a brief strategy meeting, Del and I split up. He walked to the top of a low rise that offered a 180-degree view, while I climbed halfway up the side of a low cliff.

I found a comfortable place to sit on a footstool-sized boulder. The valley floor was just ten feet below me, and a broad shelf extended six feet overhead. I could already hear the faint strains from Del's call, so I got my own out and went to work.

After fifteen minutes of fruitless squalling, I gave it a rest. In the sudden quiet that followed, some atavistic sense kicked in. The hairs stood on the back of my neck, and I felt an unnerving presence. And when a couple of pebbles fell from above, the adrenaline really kicked in.

Swiveling around on my precarious perch, I thrust the Contender upward and tried to find something in the scope. The gun was at an awkward angle, but I already had the hammer thumbed back.

I saw sudden motion in the blackness overhead, then it was gone. I didn't get a good look, but I knew bobcats weren't that big. Hairs still prickling, I quickly stood and pulled a flashlight from my fanny pack. I scrambled up the slope until I could see the top of the shelf, and then used the flashlight to make sure nothing still lurked there.

Shouting a warning to Del, I climbed over the edge and began searching for sign. In a sandy depression I spotted fresh pug marks. No mistaking the size—I'd just been visited by a mountain lion.

When Del showed up a few minutes later, we continued to search along the shelf. Other pug marks eventually appeared, and Del confirmed my suspicion.

"That's one big cat," he exclaimed. "I knew there were cougars up here, but I didn't know they'd come to a call."

Slightly spooked by the outsized feline, we moved down the mountainside and set up shop in another location a quarter-mile away. A few minutes later we had proof our visitor was still with us. By now we no longer depended on the pale red glow provided by our headlamps. Every few minutes, we'd sweep the brush with the powerful beams of our flashlights.

Twice, we spotted a pair of green eyes, and once caught a brief glimpse of the big cat itself. We finally decided we were in no real danger. The cougar wasn't looking for a super-sized meal. It was simply curious about what two humans were doing wandering around at such an ungodly hour.

We didn't get a shot at the cougar, although we certainly tried. I eventually did kill a mountain lion with a handgun, but it was several years later under entirely different circumstances.

I've given up trying to shoot toothy, fur-bearing critters at night, but I still hunt them with handguns every chance I get. But I don't use handguns exclusively. Some locales are so open and lacking in cover, it's all I can do to coax wary predators into rifle range. But whenever circumstances permit me to lure a fox, bobcat, or coyote to within forty or fifty yards, I bring along a handgun.

One problem with calling in close cover or heavy brush is that when an animal appears, he may be really packing the mail. Wary bobcats tend to pussyfoot cautiously toward the sound of calling, but foxes and coyotes often arrive on the run. Once they spot you or sense something seriously amiss, they can go through the gears in a hurry. That's the reason many brush hunters favor bigbore scatterguns. Centering a fast-stepping coyote with an open-sighted sixgun requires luck and a double helping of skill. It can (sometimes) be done, but trying the same trick with a scoped pistol may be asking too much. A 2X pistol scope offers extremely tight viewing, while a 4X or 6X scope is even harder to use.

Skilled callers who make careful use of camouflage may switch to squeaking when an animal closes in. A mouse-like squeak can freeze a predator in its tracks—but only for a moment. You'd better be ready to shoot, and shoot quickly. Once that fleeting chance passes and the critter takes off, you'll wish you had a shotgun.

While not as desirable for fast, instinctive shooting, handguns do offer some definite advantages over scatterguns. Even 10-gauge shotguns have an effective range of only forty yards— maybe fifty if you're willing to stretch the barrel. A scoped pistol

Larry Rogers with a red fox shot at eighty-five yards with a Thompson/Center Contender. Photo courtesy of Thompson/Center.

chambered for a flat-shooting rifle round like the .223, .22–250, or .243 Winchester can make things awfully hot for a yodel dog even two hundred yards (or more) downrange. When it comes to gunning varmints, handguns are more versatile than any shotgun.

I've learned from experience that winter can be a prime time for calling. When the weather is freezing and there's a layer of snow on the ground, all critters have a tough time finding something to eat. Cold adds to the hunger, so an easy meal is something a coyote, fox, or bobcat has a hard time passing up.

Calls carry far in cold air, so it's best not to get impatient too soon. Coyotes are willing to travel a fair distance to dine on disabled jack. I've sometimes seen a half-exhausted yodel dog run up a full half hour after I first began screaming the dinner call.

Winter also makes camouflage easy. There are a number of different snow-camo patterns available from manufacturers of hunting clothing. In a pinch, simply steal an old sheet from the family linen closet and head for the hills.

When you blend with the snowy terrain, it's not difficult to call hungry varmints in close. In a situation like this, almost any handgun will do. When Freedom Arms was preparing to introduce its .454 Casull revolver, I was invited to Freedom, Wyoming to hunt with one of the early prototypes.

January in Wyoming is something to experience. The motel I stayed at was freezing cold, with snow occasionally drifting through the loosely fitting door. Varmints were the only possible game available for hunting, so I'd brought my varmint calls along.

I spent one memorable morning huddled in a low line of trees. I wore insulated white pants

This trio of eastern coyotes fell to Herb Pennington's .223 Remington T/C Contender with a fourteen-inch barrel. Photo courtesy of Thompson/Center.

Winter can be a great time to call predators into handgun range, but the right camouflage is vital.

and a coat that usually kept me toasty, but they weren't up to the kind of marrow-freezing cold I'd been feeling since shortly after sunup. The sheet I had wrapped around me didn't add much protection from frostbite.

Fortunately, I got lucky early. In a big hurry for breakfast, a starving fox showed up on a dead run only minutes after I started to call. The .454 slug passed completely through the animal at thirty yards.

Firing the big, hard-kicking revolver badly stung my half-frozen hands, and my unprotected ears felt the full force of the blast. I try to wear plugs whenever I hunt with handguns, but I'd somehow forgotten to bring any along. Besides, I wanted my hearing unimpaired so I could hear snow crunch under approaching feet. The fox appeared silently out of thin air, but got an extremely noisy reception. I'd made my first kill with the big

Casull, and decided that was enough fun for one day. It was time to find a warm stove and a hot breakfast.

So what happened with the cougar I finally shot? I've never had another of these big cats answer a call, but while hunting them the traditional way in southern Utah's desert country I discovered handguns were the armament of choice. Following a pack of rangy, constantly baying hounds through sagebrush, rimrock, and stands of cedar isn't a stroll in the park. When fresh lion scent is found, the dogs take off like greyhounds chasing a mechanical rabbit. We mere humans follow on horses.

In mountain lion territory, chasing the big cats outranks any other outdoor sport. Hound owners do this every chance they get, temporarily ignoring their regular jobs to eagerly pursue their quarry. This doesn't happen just once or twice each year, but every time a cougar shows up in the general neighborhood. Dedicated

This mountain lion tom was killed with a single shot from Luverne Crosser's .30 Herrett Thompson/Center Contender. Photo courtesy of Thompson/Center.

hound men are lean, long-legged, whang-leather-tough individuals who could put a trained triathlete to shame.

Even with horses, chasing lions is exhausting. Riding hell-bent through stands of cedar and piñon trees isn't my idea of relaxing recreation. The cat often trees where horses can't follow, and then you're on your own. When this happened to me, I just had to hope that I wouldn't lose track of my guide or the dogs he was frantically following.

The only real danger is to the dogs. If a cat can't find a handy tree to climb, he may find himself cornered against a rocky cliff or in heavy brush. When this happens, dogs can get hurt. By itself, even the biggest hound is no match for a cougar's teeth and claws. So hound men hurry to reach their dogs before fur and blood start flying.

Once a cat is treed, the excitement is over. Actually shooting the animal is anticlimactic. Considering a cedar tree's low height, high-powered rifles aren't required. A handgun is ideal for this kind of work. You can carry a revolver securely holstered, where it's out of the way until needed. In a pinch, any .22 rimfire will do. I did the job with my Smith & Wesson Mountain Gun stoked with factory-loaded .44 Specials. Fired from ten feet away, a single well-placed round ended this deer-eating cat's career.

Chapter 9

HUNTING DEER WITH HANDGUNS

Deer have long been the favorite game of American hunters, whether they use high-powered rifles, bows, muzzleloaders, or handguns. These animals are ubiquitous. Huntable populations of whitetail, mule, or blacktail deer are found in every state. In many areas (like my home state of Utah), these wonderful animals can be hunted on public ground. Private landowners are increasingly likely to charge access fees.

It's still possible to get within handgun range of a good, heavy-antlered buck on public land, but these days real trophy wall-hangers are much more likely to be found on land leased by professional outfitters. If your primary focus is putting venison in the freezer, does are more plentiful and easier to hunt.

You don't need a real powerhouse handgun for hunting deer. A .41 magnum or .44 magnum revolver—or a pistol chambering any .30–30-class cartridge—can be counted on to kill deer if you limit the range to seventy-five or even a hundred yards. Longer distances call for a scoped pistol chambering flatter-shooting deer rounds like the 7mm/08 or .308.

While considerably more potent handgun cartridges like the .454 Casull, .450 Marlin, .475 Linebaugh, and .50 AE—or even

Larry Kelly shot this Montana whitetail with a J. D. Jones–customized T/C Contender in 6.5 JDJ chambering.

the .500 Smith & Wesson—can be used for hunting deer, this kind of power isn't really necessary. Opting for one of these behemoth, big-game rounds means much greater recoil and less control. At the other end of the spectrum, the .357 magnum is legal for deer hunting in many states, but it's a marginal round few serious hunters will even consider. Before carrying a handgun in the deer woods, be sure to check hunting regulations in your state for minimum cartridge requirements.

Long-barreled pistols like the T/C Encore, Contender, and Savage Striker can be as accurate as a rifle at extended ranges. Fitted with a long-eye-relief handgun scope and chambering high-intensity rifle rounds like the .308 or 7mm/08, these guns can be deadly on deer at two hundred yards or more. You'll need to rest your pistol against something solid—a tree trunk, boulder, or

Robert Donnelly shot this huge fourteen-point Maine whitetail at seventy-five yards with a T/C Contender. Photo courtesy of Thompson/Center.

This eight-point whitetail buck was taken at 132 yards by J. D. Jones with a prototype SIG-Blaser pistol.

bipod—but with a little practice you'll be able to kill deer-sized game cleanly at what was once considered "rifle-only" distances.

I've hunted deer with both kinds of handguns, but more and more I find myself toting a sixgun in the woods. What caliber? Well, I've tried the more powerful loads, but when deer season rolls around I'm more likely to carry one of the .44 magnum revolvers in my safe than any other handgun.

I have several .44 magnum sixguns to choose from. (Unlike extreme-pressure rounds like the .454 that require thick-walled, five-round cylinders, the old .44 magnum does just fine in a standard six-shot cylinder.) My battery includes a Ruger Hunter Model Super Blackhawk with weather-resistant stainless steel and Ruger's integral bases for easy scope mounting. There's also a double-action Ruger Super Redhawk, a six-inch Smith & Wesson Model 629, a Dan Wesson "Hunter Pack" featuring a .44 mag-

Chris Helms with the magnificent 9x8 mule deer buck he took with a T/C Contender in .45–70 chambering. Photo courtesy of Thompson/Center.

num revolver with interchangeable barrels, and a Taurus Model 44SS6 with a 6½-inch ported barrel.

One of my favorite trail guns is a four-inch-barreled Smith & Wesson Mountain Gun. The game laws in my state don't allow handgunning deer with a four-inch barrel, so I have yet to shoot large game with this light, handy (but hard-kicking) revolver.

The .44 magnum has plenty of punch for deer out to one hundred yards, but these days it's tough for me to put all six shots in the cylinder into an eight-inch paper plate at that distance. So when it comes to hunting deer with iron-sighted .44 magnum revolvers, I've set fifty yards as my outside limit. Remember, hunting with handguns is *supposed* to be challenging. My challenge is being skillful and patient enough to stalk within fifty yards (thirty yards is even better), and then using open sights to place the bullet where I want it to go.

DESERT MULE DEER

The first deer I took with a handgun fell to a single-action Ruger Super Blackhawk I'd purchased a few months earlier. I didn't add a scope, choosing instead to use the excellent adjustable iron sights the gun came equipped with. Well before the hunt, I burned through several hundred practice rounds of low-recoiling .44 Special loads and full-house magnum hunting fodder.

I wasn't a beginning pistoleer, though. I'd owned a number of different handguns over the years and killed my share of squirrels and jackrabbits with highly accurate .22 rimfire pistols and revolvers. But hunting deer was different. I didn't want to leave a wounded buck in the woods, so I took my shooting practice seriously. In time, I was able to put six consecutive shots into a nine-inch paper plate at seventy-five yards. That's not pinpoint precision, but I felt confident in tackling a deer if I limited my shooting to the short side of fifty yards.

The blaze orange–clad author hunting with his Ruger Super Blackhawk.

I'd planned on an extended-season hunt in Utah's Dolores Triangle. The state's general deer season ended at the end of October, but a number of permits were available on a "first-come" basis for the limited November hunt. The Dolores Triangle is located right on the border with Colorado, not far from Grand Junction. Savvy hunters who got in line first—I was among them that year—had the chance to shoot one of the monster muleys that summered in Colorado's high plateaus and wintered in the Utah desert.

I'd hunted the area with a rifle once before and knew it could produce big-bodied bucks with large, heavy antlers. As a bonus, the rut was well underway, making deer less wary as they began their search for romance. (Utah's general deer season ends well before the love bug bites.) I left for the Triangle a few days before Thanksgiving.

The weather was dry the afternoon Ken Turner and I set up camp, but when we unzipped the tent door the next morning we were greeted with fifteen inches of fresh snow. Snow continued trickling from the sky as we chained up and drove two miles to the area we'd decided to hunt. It was slippery going. Melting snow had already turned the dry, desert dust into a thick, gooey layer of muck.

Leaving the truck, we parted company. Ken and his rifle went north, while I headed south into the white-frosted sage-brush desert.

Aware of the limitations of my open-sighted .44 magnum, I found a likely spot close to a trail that had apparently been used earlier that morning. The still-falling snow hadn't completely erased the tracks, which looked like they'd been made by at least two or three deer. I was gambling that more deer would be along soon.

Mule deer have the knack of finding the path of least resistance, and where one goes, others are likely to follow. When deer are in the neighborhood, a recently used trail is likely to see additional use soon. Anyhow, it was snowing too hard to see very far, so there was no point in looking for deer in the distance and hoping to plan a stalk.

There was plenty of sagebrush to break up my outline, so I sat in the snow with my back snuggled against a large clump of sage, then settled down to wait. I was hoping for a short-range opportunity and the chance to shoot from a solid sitting position. I needed all the help I could get.

An hour slowly passed, and the snow stopped falling. Before I had time to become impatient, I spotted a pair of does working toward me down the now-invisible trail. I didn't want anything blocking my shot, so I wasn't hiding behind the sagebrush. Instead, I sat in front with my back to the sage. I was in plain sight, but my outline was nicely broken up. A dusting of snow on my jacket and pants added to the camouflage.

I can't count the times I've had deer pass within a few feet of me, even though I sat in full view wearing blaze orange clothing. Remaining motionless is the key. If deer don't see movement, they're seldom alarmed by color alone. However, in this flat white terrain, wary deer would quickly spot any motion I made.

Hoping a buck wasn't far behind the does, I allowed them to pass. Barely glancing in my direction, they continued their unhurried progress through the snow. Sure enough, a big desert muley soon appeared on the trail. The buck displayed thick-beamed antlers — only three points to a side, but wide and heavy.

When I spotted the animal, I slowly eased the Ruger into shooting position and quietly thumbed the hammer back. Then I froze in place. The buck was only thirty-five yards away when I settled the front sight just behind his shoulder and squeezed the trigger. I don't remember hearing the

The author dropped this nice Utah buck with an open-sighted .44 magnum Ruger Super Blackhawk on his first handgun hunt for deer.

blast or feeling any recoil. I was so totally focused on the animal that I was aware of nothing else.

After two quick leaps, the animal collapsed. No second shot was needed. The 240-grain factory softpoint had done its job. I've killed many mule deer in a lifetime of hunting, but none with greater satisfaction.

TEXAS WHITETAIL

"What're you doing next November?" were the first words Larry Weishuhn said when I answered the phone. Larry is a fellow writer who also does public relations work for Thompson/Center. Before I could answer, he added, "How'd you like to come to the Nail Ranch and give the new G2 Contender a workout on Texas whitetails?"

At the time, the G2 Contender was just being introduced. And the chance to use a brand-new handgun was a bonus. I'd acquired my first Contender more than twenty years earlier and had used it to hunt deer, coyotes, and a few other critters. However, I'd never hunted whitetails with my single-shot Contender. In more years of hunting than I'd care to remember, the vast majority of deer I'd killed had been mule deer. I welcomed the chance to hunt Texas whitetails. I was also curious to see what changes had been made in the new G2 Contender.

The hunt took place on the 56,000-acre Nail Ranch near Abilene, in west-central Texas. The century-old working cattle ranch is famous for big bucks, and I was hoping for a chance to take a trophy whitetail.

November finally arrived and Larry met me at the airport. We stopped at Wal-Mart long enough to pick up a Texas hunting license, then headed for the ranch and a chuck-wagon supper. The hunting operation was under the direction of Craig Winters, the Nail Ranch wildlife manager.

After breakfast the next morning, Larry and I met Tim Mariner, our guide. He'd drive the truck and attend to the rattling chores. Cameraman Mike Pellagatti also came along to film Larry's hunt for an upcoming Thompson/Center television show.

As we climbed in the truck, Larry handed me the .30–30 G2 Contender I'd hunt with. It was the first time I'd seen the scoped gun. "I sighted it in yesterday," he said. "It's dead-on at a hundred yards. If you want to check the zero, we can swing by the rifle range before we start hunting."

I passed on the shooting range, as I trusted Larry's expertise and didn't want to waste that important first half hour of hunting time. I broke the Contender's action and climbed into the passenger seat of the four-wheel-drive truck. I was to have the first shot if we spotted game; Mike and Larry sat in back. With the gun in my lap and three rounds of 150-grain Winchester factory loads in my breast pocket, I was ready to hunt.

Not ten minutes later, Tim stood on the brake and pointed to something in the brush ninety yards away. "See him?" he asked. "The one on the left is a good ten-pointer! That's a shootable buck!"

I fumbled a cartridge from my pocket and slipped out of the truck. My buck stood between two trees, partially screened by brush. I was wishing for a sandbag as I leaned across the hood and tried to steady the gun on target. Then I discovered that Larry had set the variable T/C scope at 7X when he'd sighted in. I stupidly hadn't thought to check the magnification. It took me several seconds to find the animal in the long-eye-relief scope's tight field of view.

The buck was facing directly away when I finally found him in the scope. I didn't want to take a rear-end shot with a .30–30 softpoint traveling at pistol-barrel velocities. Then the buck took a half-step forward, turning his head to look back at me. I had a sliver of shoulder to shoot at, so I pressed the trigger. Apparently unhurt, the buck bolted into the brush.

I wasn't as steady as I should have been, and I'd heard no satisfying *whock*. It looked like a clean miss, but Tim and I circled wide, trying to get ahead of the animal. Once we were in place and ready, Larry and Mike slowly walked to where we'd last seen the deer. There was no sign of blood. A few minutes later we watched the obviously unscathed buck run over a distant ridgetop.

Cussing myself for the lost chance, I broke the Contender's action and cranked the scope to its lowest magnification, 2 1/2X. Mistakes like this are always embarrassing, particularly when others are watching.

After riding a few more miles, I told Tim I'd really rather walk than hunt from the seat of a truck. I've put a lot of hard

miles on my boots hunting mule deer in desert and mountain country and wasn't accustomed to being driven around. Tim then explained the realities of hunting the nearly one-hundred-square-mile ranch.

"During a three-day hunt, we'll typically show you *at least* three hundred

Binoculars are a big help in finding bucks, even at handgunning range.

deer," he said. "Maybe one-third will be bucks. The only way to see that many deer is to cover lots of ground. But you won't be spending all your time in the truck. We'll drive to different hotspots where the deer hang out, then leave the truck and walk."

The Nail Ranch has no high fences and releases no deer on its property. It's strictly fair-chase hunting all the way. This is a fully operational cattle ranch with a healthy population of native whitetail, wild hogs, turkeys, and other game.

"Here's our first honey hole," Tim said, stopping the truck. While Larry and Mike legged it in another direction, Tim and I walked to a low hill at the edge of a distant line of trees. Once we found a likely spot, I sat with my back to a clump of brush that broke my outline. Tim sat a few yards behind me, antlers in hand. I steadied the Contender on my Steady-Stix bipod, and Tim began clashing the set of antlers he carried.

I knew rattling was a widely used tactic in whitetail country, but I wasn't prepared for how quickly my guide got results. Less than a minute after Tim began working his antlers, a buck charged out of the brush, head high and spoiling for a fight. I was startled by its sudden appearance.

The author is ready for action as guide Tim Mariner rattles up a whitetail buck.

The buck was a decent one, but it's eight-point rack didn't interest me much after I'd missed the big ten-pointer.

Tim's rattling continued until the buck finally became suspicious and ran off. Successful rattling didn't seem to require a lot of skill. As far as I could tell, you simply kept clashing the horns together until you saw deer or decided to move on. Tim kept at it for another five or six minutes and a second buck appeared—a twin of the first. We decided it was time to trek back to the truck.

The rest of the day followed the same pattern. We'd drive twenty minutes, then park and walk a quarter-mile or more to the next rattling spot. When we didn't set up in brush or trees, we'd sit behind waist-high clumps of cactus. Inadvertently brushing against prickly pear gave me a number of painful hitchhikers, and I began paying more attention to where I sat. Tim managed to call in deer almost everywhere we set up shop.

We saw lots of deer, but passed on all of them for a variety of reasons—mostly relating to antler size and the fact that it was the

Handgun hunters must blend into the background when calling deer.

first day of the hunt. The only shot fired after my miss was when Larry spotted a coyote chasing mice forty yards from the truck. Larry rolled down the window and ended the yodel dog's career with his Thompson/Center muzzleloader.

Riding back to the bunkhouse in the growing darkness, I welcomed the chance to rest my legs in the truck. I'd done more than enough walking that day. I was tired—but it was a *good* kind of tired. My only regret was missing that ten-pointer in the early morning light.

I was beginning to nod off when Tim urgently nudged me and pointed out the window. "Look! I think I see some interesting antlers!"

I could see a shadowy animal running parallel with the truck, eighty yards from the road. In the gathering darkness, my eyes had a hard time making out horns. But when Tim slammed on the brakes and roared, "Shoot that buck!" I didn't stop to argue. The tone of his voice told me we were onto something special. Jamming a round into the gun, I jumped out of the truck.

Three quick steps took me to the barbed-wire fence alongside the road. Cushioning the Contender with my hand, I steadied it atop a fencepost. I saw impressive-looking antlers as I found the deer in my scope, but I didn't have time to count points. The buck paused, standing briefly silhouetted against a blood-red sunset as the crosshairs settled behind its shoulder. This was one shot I didn't want to miss, and the buck dropped in its tracks at the crack of the shot.

Larry pounded me on the shoulder as I climbed the fence and hurried to the dead animal. "You knew what you were doing when you missed that buck this morning," he chortled. "That was the second-luckiest thing you've done today!"

My one regret was that it was nearly full dark. Flash photography couldn't capture the magnificence of the fallen fourteen-point buck. As Mike took several photos with my 35mm camera, Tim told me not to worry about picture quality. "We'll get you some decent photos," he said. "Wait and see."

Back at the ranch, we unloaded the deer from the truck and carried it into a large freezing room. The animal was posed in a head-up position, with its antlers wired to supports overhead. The head scored 163 points and change—the best whitetail buck I'd ever killed.

"He'll be frozen stiff by morning," Tim assured me. "There'll be plenty of time to take better photos tomorrow."

After another dutch-oven breakfast the next morning, the four of us again boarded the truck and headed for deer country.

Carrying my camera, I followed Larry, Mike, and Tim to several different locations, where Tim repeatedly rattled good bucks into easy muzzleloader range. Larry aimed at each buck, following it with the sights as Mike filmed the action. I kept waiting for the shot, but

The author shot this fourteen-point Texas whitetail with a .30–30 T/C G2 Contender.

Larry wanted everything just right before ending the hunt. I expected him to shoot one particular ten-point buck that stopped to pose for the camera, but sun glare blinded his scope just before he tripped the trigger. Larry showed surprising patience, passing up several shots I'd have taken.

Late the following day—the last of the hunt—Larry was finally filmed shooting his buck just as the light was failing.

The G2 Contender I used during the hunt had a lot in common with the aging .30–30 Contender in my gun safe at home. The new gun is visually similar to the T/C Encore. The Encore is beefier and handles stiffer loads, but both have smooth receivers with projections extending on either side of chamber. The original Contender has a slab-sided action that sports some modest engraving.

In a major change that was long overdue, the new G2 Contender can be repeatedly cocked and uncocked without opening the action. This eliminated the one great annoyance Contender fans previously had to deal with.

All the Contenders (and Encores) I've used over the years have delivered excellent accuracy.

The G2 Contender is roughly the same size and heft (3½ pounds with a 12-inch tube) as the old Contender and accepts all existing Contender barrels. A patented automatic hammer-block safety guards against accidental firing.

Just as whitetails are the number-one choice of American sportsmen during rifle season, deer are a favorite target for hunting handgunners. Whitetail, blacktail, or mule deer are readily available throughout the United States. There's no need to bankrupt your savings account by trekking to Alaska or booking an African safari. Hunting deer with a handgun is a challenging, rewarding pursuit anyone can afford.

Chapter 10

PISTOLING PRONGHORNS

While Wyoming is pronghorn heaven, I live right next door in Utah, which has its own native population of western antelope. And even though I admired these graceful, incredibly fleet-footed animals as I grew up, pronghorn hunting still held a mystical lure.

I'd read countless magazine articles that detailed how hard pronghorn were to hunt. There were so many stories describing long-range shooting that I honestly believed you needed a tack-driving, flat-shooting rifle mounting a two-liter-sized scope to have any hope of killing a pronghorn buck.

A few weeks before heading to Wyoming in search of my first antelope (yeah, the Cowboy state *does* have more pronghorn than Utah, and by a wide margin), I had an experience that started me scratching my head.

My buddies and I were walking through the sagebrush desert of northeastern Utah only a few miles from the Wyoming border, hunting for sage grouse. These big, slow-flying birds aren't hard to hunt. Once you find a flock in a particular place at a particular time, you can usually return to the same spot year after year and have birds in the air within twenty or thirty minutes—if you're careful not to overshoot the population. They're hard-wired creatures of habit.

We hunted them by forming a skirmish line with shooters thirty yards or so apart. These hunts typically featured regular volleys of gunfire, followed by several minutes of silence as the hunters regrouped to follow the fleeing birds. It makes for a fairly noisy day with shots ringing out periodically.

So I was startled when a band of maybe a dozen antelope wandered through our skirmish line, calmly passing within twenty yards. Hadn't they just heard us shooting? Couldn't they see our guns? I began wondering if pronghorn really were all that wary. Or maybe they were smarter than I imagined and knew pronghorn season hadn't yet begun.

Later, I bought a Wyoming hunting license and drove to my designated unit. The friend who'd planned to go with me had something come up and was forced to stay home. This would be a solo hunt.

Driving along a graveled road that cut through the vast Wyoming prairie, I spotted a small band of pronghorn settling in for a late morning nap just below the crest of a distant hillside. Stopping my truck, I took a long look through my binocular. Sure enough, each and every animal was looking directly back at me. Okay, they have superb, long-range vision. I already knew that. And there was at least one decent buck in the bunch—maybe even two.

I also knew I couldn't approach very closely, even in a slow-moving truck. And I knew there'd be an alert doe standing sentinel while the others dozed in the sagebrush. Wouldn't there? That's what all the magazine articles had said.

The road curved right, then passed behind the hill. I drove steadily along until I was safely out of sight. Then I stopped the truck again and focused my binocular on the crest. I saw no ante-lope. Where *was* that sentinel doe?

Nothing ventured, nothing gained—so I slowly drove to the base of the hill just below where I thought the pronghorns were resting on the other side. Quietly stepping from the truck, being careful not to slam the door, I pointed my binocular upwards and carefully searched the brush for some sign of a lookout. Again, I found none.

Hardly believing my luck, I climbed to just below the top of the hill. Then I dropped to my knees, and pushing my rifle before me, gingerly crawled over the crest.

Expecting to see only the backsides of fleeing pronghorn in the distance, I was startled to see a big, black eye staring at me through the sagebrush. The doe unfolded her legs and stood up, and several other antelope followed suit. Then the buck I'd hoped for rose from the brush, eyeing me in alarm.

A second later I had him in my scope and a 100-grain 6mm Remington bullet was on its way. It didn't have far to go—the buck fell back to the ground just fifteen long paces away. The rest of the herd flowed down the hill in frantic flight.

This may seem like a long way to go to make a point about pistoling pronghorns, but it was the first step in my decision to do just that a few years later. At first, I was absolutely convinced this too-easy hunt had been a once-in-lifetime fluke. The following year it took a much longer shot to drop a 14½-inch buck—sixty yards!

I've taken a double handful of pretty nice pronghorns over the years with rifle and handgun alike. None were farther than a hundred yards from the muzzle when I fired. I killed four bucks with a rifle before switching to a scoped Contender. If it hadn't been for my earlier close-range success when carrying a rifle, I may not have had the confidence to leave the long gun home in favor of a single-shot pistol.

In subsequent years, I had the opportunity to hunt pronghorns with the late Bob Milek (his look-alike son is following in his father's footsteps). As anyone who read the many hundreds of magazine articles he wrote knows, Bob was a dedicated handgun hunter and an early champion of the Thompson/Center Contender.

During our hunt, I watched Bob drop a 15½-inch buck at 140 yards with a round from his scoped, single-shot pistol. He probably could've stalked closer, but why bother? For Bob, 140 yards was practically point-blank range. It took some skill to make the shot, but it wasn't a demanding distance for the right kind of handgun. I knew Bob had taken countless game, large and small, at considerably longer range, and under much more difficult circumstances. But 140 yards was hardly the kind of barrel-stretching distance I'd read about.

The author's .30–30 Contender has plenty of reach, but he's never had to shoot a pronghorn at extreme range—yet.

How do you get within good handgun range of pronghorn? The truth is, it really isn't all that hard. Antelope see incredibly well at long distances and are wary and astonishingly fast—but they can be fooled.

Many times I've watched road-bound riflemen pile out of a truck and start blazing away at a pronghorn on the far horizon. And I've seen too many antelope turned into three-legged cripples because some hunter thought a high-powered rifle and scope could substitute for judgment and shooting skill.

One reason pronghorn have the reputation for requiring long-range marksmanship is the surprising way most hunters approach them. Sadly, many sportsmen like to hunt from the comfort of their truck, seldom walking more than fifty yards from the road to shoot. Conditioned by years of this kind of hunting, antelope become leery of roads. They do their best to avoid them as soon as the first shots of the season ring out.

If you stick to the roads, pausing now and then to glass distant bucks, you'll probably see lots of animals. Of course, they'll see you, too. Stalking an alerted antelope from the road can be done, but it isn't an easy task. It usually involves hundreds of yards of duck walking and belly crawling to have much chance of success. That's more sweaty, painful work than most road warriors are willing to do.

Several years ago I discovered one key to handgunning pronghorn without becoming exhausted or incredibly dirty. In company of some other nimrods, I was hunting in southern Wyoming with Burris Scope's John McCarty. It was distressing to watch two of the hunters attempt 450-yard shots. Their marksmanship skills weren't up to the task, and when the dust cleared both bucks were running as hard as they could, each with one leg missing.

Abandoning the wounded animals, the other hunters roared off down the road, looking for fresh targets. John and I asked someone in our party to circle around and drive us toward the

Larry Kelly shot this desert pronghorn with a J. D. Jones Hand Cannon.

badlands in which the wounded animals had just vanished. We wanted to go where the road didn't, so the driver dropped us off about a mile away.

Fifteen minutes of walking brought us to the area we were looking for. Except for being awfully dry and rocky, it was like a mini-Eden. Small bands of pronghorn were everywhere, and those we saw didn't seem too badly spooked by our presence. Using the cover of a shallow arroyo, we did our best to remain out of sight. At one point, we hunkered down behind a rocky outcropping while fourteen antelope walked single file past us just ten yards away.

We spent two highly enjoyable hours in the badlands watching both three-legged and four-legged pronghorn. Eventually John shot a nice buck that wandered by some sixty yards away. I took its twin at just thirty-five yards—perfect handgun range.

On another occasion, I'd left my companions and set out to wander through the sagebrush-studded desert. I was enjoying my

Kurt Williams shot this sixteen-plus-inch Wyoming antelope at 225 yards with a T/C Contender.

J. Scott Olmstead used a T/C G2 Contender chambered for the 7–30 Waters to shoot this buck at 130 yards. Photo courtesy of Thompson/Center.

stroll and didn't hurry. Whenever I spotted pronghorn in the distance, I'd stop to examine them with my binocular. Two or three hunters stand out in desert country, but a lone hunter making even a minimal effort to avoid skylines and keep out of sight has a greater chance of avoiding notice.

It was midafternoon, and my canteen was running low when it happened. A trio of hunters some eight hundred yards away were slowly moving in my direction. Lowering my binocular, I suddenly noticed a small band of antelope directly between us. One looked like a nice buck—not a bragging trophy, but sporting black, curving horns that I estimated at around fourteen inches. The pronghorns were in no hurry. They moved at the same pace the hunters had set. And like the hunters, they were moving my way.

I watched the pronghorns from behind a tall clump of sagebrush next to a barbed-wire fence that was directly in their path. When the animals reached the fence, they'd have to turn either right or left. If they turned right, they would pass by within easy range of the .30–30 Contender I carried.

I dropped into a comfortable sitting position and settled down to wait. It was even money whether I'd get a shot, but if they came my way I was ready. I did my best to remain perfectly motionless. A few short minutes later, I spotted movement out of the corner of my eye. Quietly thumbing the hammer to full-cock, I kept my head turned forward, hoping the buck would appear in my peripheral vision.

Suddenly there he was, barely fifteen feet away. Talk about dead-cinch shots! I was in a rock-solid shooting position and the animal was so close I saw mostly hide in the scope. It was the second-closest kill I'd ever made on large game.

I didn't really need the scoped Contender. I'd brought it along in case I had to shoot at one hundred yards or more. One of my open-sighted revolvers would have been a better choice.

I love hunting pronghorns. I also prefer hunting them with a pistol, although I haven't yet begun carrying an iron-sighted revolver in antelope country. Maybe part of me still believes what I read all those years ago. In spite of my experiences hunting pronghorns up close, maybe I *will* have to take a long-range shot one day.

Chapter 11

HUNTING LARGE NORTH AMERICAN GAME

I remember when hunting anything larger than rabbits or squirrels with a handgun was considered a novelty. During the 1950s, I was thrilled by the adventures of a writer named Goerg. He was the first to take a bigbore sixgun to Alaska in search of bear and other outsized game. He also pioneered the use of scope sights on handguns.

Goerg blazed a trail others eventually followed. While the .44 magnum was (and remains) strictly a short-range proposition, hunters soon began carrying revolvers chambered for this fine sixgun cartridge in the deer woods. A few used the big .44 to hunt even larger game.

In the days when the .44 magnum was the epitome of handgun power, some Alaskan hunting and fishing guides toted .44 sixguns as insurance against big, bad-tempered bears. The .480 Ruger, .454 Casull, .450 Marlin, .475 Linebaugh, and .500 Smith & Wesson revolvers available today are far better choices. But a lot of awfully big critters have been taken with .44 magnums. Call me a wimp, but I'd personally think twice before intentionally using

Mark Hampton shot this ten-foot Alaskan brown bear at eighty-two yards with a T/C Contender pistol in .375 caliber using 270-grain Hornady bullets.

Larry Weishuhn used a .30–06 Thompson/Center Encore pistol to drop this record-book Alaskan caribou.

This bull moose fell to Gerald Kraft's .44 magnum Smith & Wesson Model 29 with Mag-na-ported barrel.

Robert Dillon killed this mountain goat with a .375 Win. T/C Contender at 110 yards. It's the No. 1 SCI (Safari Club International) handgun record.

one to keep a brown bear at bay. Having one of the new super magnums in my hand would make me infinitely more confident about surviving a grizzly attack.

If you're going to hunt moose, elk, or grizzlies with a handgun, one of these super-potent cylinder guns is often the best way to go. Some customized single-shot pistols may match them in killing power, but chances are you'll need to fire more than once to get the job done.

While these super-magnum sixguns are great for hunting large game, recoil discourages extended shooting sessions. A fair amount of practice is required to learn to control these hard-kicking revolvers and develop acceptable hunting accuracy. However, fire too many of the potent rounds they chamber during the same shooting session and flinching quickly becomes a factor.

Countless sportsmen (and sportswomen) have successfully hunted North America's biggest game animals with a handgun. Here are some accounts from those who have:

TED NUGENT'S .44 MAGNUM CARIBOU

Rock legend Ted Nugent is a noted handgunner, author, and gun-rights advocate.

My first Alaskan safari came in September 1977. It represented a hunting kid's dream come true, and I practiced almost daily the entire year before the trip. My carry gun at the time was a beautiful S&W M29, 6½-inch Mag-na-ported .44 mag, and I bet I went through at least a thousand rounds of Remington 240-grain softpoints that summer. I'd set up life-sized paper deer targets at 50, 100, 150, and 200 yards in my fields and woods and would go out there with binoculars and bags of ammo. From a sitting position with my forearms resting on my knees, I became deadly at all ranges with that combination.

The expert gunsmiths at Larry Kelly's Mag-na-port Arms did a great tuning job, and I knew that trigger like I know my Gibson Byrdland guitar neck. All that shooting developed intense confidence, and it all came together on my third day in the Alaskan wilderness.

George Faerber was my guide. We were deep in the Alaskan bush, and we had a riot every day. We glassed lots of caribou and black bear and moose from our tent camp on a magnificent mountainside, and had many good stalks.

Wishing to use my bow on the big game, I wore my big blue Smith & Wesson in a Lawman shoulder rig with a double speed pouch on my belt. Of course, as always, my pockets were full of loose cartridges as we set out in pursuit of caribou.

Following twisting, humping ridges and breaks in the tundra, my two-mile stalk came to an abrupt end when I peeked over a hummock at four gorgeous Barren Ground bull caribou seventy yards out. They saw me, too. They lifted their heads high, flung their enormous antlers back, and trotted down and around a willow-choked ravine.

The biggest of the bunch was a real dandy to this flatlander, so I dropped my bow and hustled to the high point before me just as the bulls cleared the line of brush. I sat down in the wet lichens, and in a ballistician ballet, cold blue pointed straight at the running beasts from solid arms on solid knees. The red front ramp of the Smith's front sight swung slow and smooth toward the largest bull's chest, and at about 150 yards the other bulls opened up and exposed the big boy. The hammer came back, I took a deep breath, and the revolver leapt in my hands.

A resonant *whomp* came back to me as the bull's head dropped, 240 grains of lead smashing his shoulder bone and penetrating both lungs. He crashed face-first into the tundra as the other caribou vanished into the wild. I looked back at George through my binoculars and saw him hold a clenched fist skyward, as pleased as I was over the instant kill on the good bull. He was a handgun hunter himself, and we celebrated with the Great Spirit that night with fresh-roasted backstrap filets in the lap of God.

HANDGUNNING ELK WITH LARRY KELLY

Larry Kelly, of Mag-na-port fame, was one of the early proponents of handgun hunting. He generously shares several of his many handgunning adventures in this book.

"Several years ago, my brother-in-law shot a 6x6 bull elk in Idaho with a .44 magnum Ruger revolver," Larry Kelly recalled. "Inspired by his example, I hunted hard the next fifteen years without success. I saw plenty of cows and forkhorns, but never got within handgun range of a good, mature bull.

"Elk soon became an obsession," he said. "I'd failed to score for fifteen straight years, but I wanted a big bull worse than ever. Then I got the chance to hunt New Mexico's Mescalero Apache reservation, which is home to a lot of fine elk, and has a reputation for producing big bulls. The hunt would be costly, but I hoped it'd be worth it.

"My Apache guide and I began riding at daylight, and within a few hours I knew he wasn't an experienced hunter," Larry said. "It was soon apparent I was simply being taken on a horseback ride. Instead of making suggestions, he kept asking me where *I* wanted to go. Some guide! The only view I had of a four-legged animal was of the rear end of the horse in front of me.

"At my insistent request, I was assigned a different guide the following day. Roy, a twenty-year-old Apache, was a welcome change. He loved to hunt—and what's more, knew how to do it. By 5:30 that morning, we were in a large valley listening to the whistles and grunts of nearby elk. It was still dark, and the animals sounded right on top of us.

"Months before the hunt, I'd talked with J. D. Jones," Kelly said. "When J. D. told me about necking a .444 Marlin case down to .375 and chambering the cartridge in a Contender barrel, I thought he was crazy. At the same time, I'd been having a run of bad luck hunting with my .44 magnums. Part of the problem was that I couldn't see the sights as well as I once did. I didn't want to switch to a rifle, so a scoped .375 handgun began sounding better.

"I tested a new .375 JDJ with the pistol resting over the hood of my truck," Kelly said. "After shooting 345-, 270-, and 300-grain loads in a thirty-mile-per-hour wind and grouping each string into a six-inch circle at 110 yards, I was sold on the gun. It was plenty accurate, had power to spare, and wasn't really punishing to shoot. I decided to try one on the elk hunt I had planned.

"Apparently sensing our presence, the animals were beginning to get stirred up," Kelly remembered. "We could hear a bull we knew was close, but it still wasn't light enough to see. We stayed put, and the trees before us finally began taking shape. It slowly grew lighter, and Roy suddenly nudged me. 'Get ready,' he whispered.

"I still couldn't see anything. I looked for something nearby to rest the pistol on, but couldn't find anything suitable, so I simply put my back against a tree. 'Hit him!' Roy repeatedly urged. 'I still can't see him!' I answered. I cocked the .375, and Roy again said, 'Hit him! Hit him *now*! He's a good one!'

"Suddenly I saw the bull moving in the trees. Raising the Contender, I picked out an opening and waited for the elk to fill it. When he did, I centered the Leupold 2X scope's crosshairs at the back edge of his shoulder and squeezed the trigger.

"I heard the distinct *whock*, and the animal disappeared from sight. Hurrying to the spot, which was seventy yards away, I

After fifteen straight years of going home empty-handed, Larry Kelly took this elk with a Mag-na-ported T/C in .375 JDJ chambering.

found the dead bull. No second shot was needed. I finally had my 6 × 6 elk!"

BROWN BEARS DON'T BOTHER TO KNOCK

"The first time I went handgunning for Alaskan bear, I had a great time," said Larry Kelly. "Only problem was, I came home empty-handed. I'd made the prideful mistake of passing up some pretty fair boars simply because I wanted a bigger one. As a result, I hadn't even pulled a trigger.

"As my single-engine plane landed at Cold Bay a few years later, I vowed to have fun and shoot a bear, even if it didn't make the record book," Kelly recalled. "Outfitter Clark Engle met me at the landing strip. I'd hunted with him before and was glad to see him again. He introduced me to Larry Rivers, who would fly me to camp. There I met California hunter George Wells, who was sharing the camp facilities. He would be guided by Joe Flores, while Bob Gerlack would be my guide.

"Three days later, George shot an 8½-foot bear, firing three rounds from his .460 Weatherby Magnum before the boar went down for good," Kelly said. "I began to worry about how my .44 magnum revolver would do against one of these big, tough animals. If it wasn't up to the job, I could be in trouble. The following morning, George and his guide left for caribou country, leaving the camp to Bob and myself.

"Our hunting tactics were to climb a high point and study the surrounding area with binoculars and spotting scope. Once we located a decent bear, we'd study the terrain and plan our stalk. A good guide knows the terrain and is familiar with the habits of bears. It pays to listen to his advice.

"After eight days of hard hunting, we spotted a large, dark bear. We watched him moving around the mountainside. He eventually crossed a hilltop and disappeared.

"'I think he's going to bed down,' Bob said. 'If he does, he'll stay there the rest of the day. Let's go after him.'

"Three hours later we struggled up the hill the bear had disappeared behind. I'd been shivering with cold before we started hiking, but I was now sweating rivers. Bob suggested we make our stalk around the left side of the hill. I wanted to go right. Bob argued that if we went that direction, the bear would hear us and disappear before we were close enough to shoot.

"Grumbling, I finally agreed to Bob's plan," Larry said. "I wasn't happy, and Bob knew it. But I respected his experience. After all, Bob knew a lot more about hunting bears than I did.

"As we neared the top of the hill, Bob whispered, 'No more talking!' A few minutes later, he indicated that I should get my gun ready. I was carrying a prototype version of the Stalker revolver I planned to produce and market.

"The Stalker is basically a stainless-steel Ruger Super Blackhawk with its 10½-inch factory barrel cut to 8⅜ inches, re-crowned, then given the Mag-na-port treatment. Vents cut just behind the muzzle by electrical discharge machining (EDM) reduce recoil by forty percent and reduce muzzle jump. The gun wears a Leupold M8–2X handgun scope in SSK Industries' extremely sturdy three-ring mount. It's a hunting gun, pure and simple.

"When I failed to immediately unsling the Stalker from my shoulder, Bob again hissed, 'Get that gun ready!' I wasted no time in complying. We eased forward a few more feet, and Bob silently pointed ahead.

"Instead of napping below us, the bear was loping up a hillside sixty yards away. Quickly dropping to a sitting position, I rested the Stalker against a boulder, buffering it with my hand. Centering the scope on the bear's shoulder, I carefully squeezed the trigger.

"Before I could cock the single-action .44 again, the bear dropped and rolled down the hill," Kelly said. "Our view was blocked by another boulder. We watched intently for a couple of minutes, then Bob said he'd go down for a look. Meanwhile, I kept my gun at the ready.

"The bear looked stone dead, but Bob asked me to come down and administer an insurance shot. As we struggled to move the bear into position for photos and skinning, Bob said, 'He's big! I think over eight feet.' As we worked, he kept revising his estimate. In the end, the bear squared 9 feet, 8 inches—a *big* bear! His 27½-inch skull missed the Boone & Crockett minimum by a bare half-inch. The .240-grain Hornady FMJ bullet had entered behind the animal's shoulder and penetrated the heart. A one-shot kill!

"We didn't know it, but our adventure with bears had only begun," Kelly recalled. "Back at camp, a storm weathered us in for the next four days. The weather was just beginning to improve as I stepped outside to relieve myself. Glancing at the beach just thirty yards away, I was startled to see a bear.

"I hollered at Bob, who grabbed his camera and joined me. He took a picture, and the bear suddenly ran toward our shack. We thought he'd run past the cabin, but Bob darted inside for his .375 H&H rifle, while I reached for the .44 magnum S&W revolver on my hip.

"Bob put a round over the bear's head to scare him off," Kelly said. "That stopped him for a moment—by now he was just fifteen yards downhill from us. The bear started for us again, and Bob fired a second shot at his feet. No sale. The animal just kept on coming.

"We frantically backed into the shack, and the bear followed us in. Bob's rifle jammed, and he backed into a Coleman stove, knocking it to the floor. Moving to the left, I tipped the old wood stove over in a cloud of soot.

"The bear started through the door, and I put a .44 magnum slug just under his chin. It didn't seem to faze him. I put a second bullet into his chest just as Bob got his rifle working and joined the fray.

"By now the bear was turning and trying to back out the door, but we both continued firing as fast as we could. As the bear finally swapped ends, I put my last two rounds low into his back. Bob's rifle clicked on an empty chamber.

"Out of ammo, I grabbed my .375 JDJ Thompson/Center Contender. The bear managed to reach the beach before my last shot put him down. Reloading all our guns, we gingerly approached. The bear was dead.

"Counting our empty brass, we learned that we'd managed to fire a total of sixteen times," Kelly said. "Fourteen of the shots had found bear. I was only glad the boar I'd shot four days earlier hadn't been so tough!

The brown bear that invaded Larry Kelly's cabin squared 9 feet, 8 inches. Photo courtesy of Larry Kelly.

"We determined the bear was in good health and hadn't been injured. The charge hadn't been provoked. We finally decided the bear had visited the shack before and had returned to look for food."

PIECE OF CAKE SHEEP

A number of years ago, Larry Kelly booked an Alaskan hunt that included black bear, grizzly, moose, and sheep. "Even now, I can't remember how sheep got on the itinerary," he said "I'd suffered from bilharzia, a disease that really knocks your pins from under you. Because of this illness, I'd canceled nearly twenty hunts. I wasn't sure how I'd hold up on a sheep mountain.

"After landing in the heart of the Chugiak Mountains, I looked up at the peak we'd be hunting on, turned to my friend Jim Herbert and said, 'Oh, my god!'

"'Don't worry about it,' was his response. 'It'll be a piece of cake.'

"He then introduced me to Duane—a typical Alaskan guide about thirty years old with legs all the way up to his neck. I asked him about the other sheep hunters he'd just been guiding, and he said, 'All gone. They just couldn't take it.' I turned angrily to Jim, who again repeated, 'Don't worry, Kelly, it's gonna be a piece of cake.'

"After three days of hard climbing, we were only three-quarters of the way up the mountain. I was ready to kill Jim. I was thoroughly, totally, completely exhausted. I begged Jim and the guide to leave me and go on ahead. 'I quit,' I groaned. 'Can't go any farther. Please leave me to die in peace.'

"'We'll stop for a rest,' Duane said. I promptly fell down and started napping while they began glassing for sheep. A half hour later I woke up and groggily crawled to the top of the rise. There I dozed again until Jim nudged my ribs and said, 'We see two rams!'

"Tired and sore, I could hardly crawl to the spotting scope. They pointed to a pair of sheep lying near a glacier, on the other side of the mountain.

"'Too far,' I moaned. 'I'd never make it there and back.'

"'Piece of cake,' Jim said.

"While I realized this could be my last sheep hunt, I couldn't have cared less," Kelly recalled.

"An hour later, we were five hundred yards from the rams," he said. "We were at a dead end, facing a sheer dropoff. We couldn't possibly get any closer, which meant returning back to where we'd just been. Jim already had the second stalk planned. 'Just work down that rock slide, then move over to that ridge, then . . . ' I remember thinking, 'Maybe if my gun accidentally went off or I stood up and waved, the sheep would run away.'

"When Duane and I finally worked our way to within two hundred yards of the rams, I felt a cool breeze on my backside. Looking down, I saw the rocks we'd been climbing over had ripped my pants to shreds. I was still breathing hard when the two rams looked directly at me. The guide said, 'Shoot! They're about to run!'

"I was carrying a Mag-na-ported T/C Contender barreled for J. D. Jones's flat-shooting 6.5 JDJ cartridge," Kelly said. "The scope's crosshairs were moving all over the place, but I finally steadied the gun down and fired. Instead of falling or rolling down the hill, the animal startled me by taking off running. I hurriedly reloaded, firing two, three, four more times. Finally the ram went down. We later discovered the sheep had been hit with my first and last shots.

"Duane caped out the magnificent full-curl ram, while I rested and wondered how I'd make it back to camp. Jim had long since headed to spike camp, and would be waiting if and when we arrived. My pack was filled with both our gear, while Duane's held the meat, cape, and horns. It was 8:00 PM before we began sidehilling down the steep mountainside.

"By midnight my Mini Mag flashlight was still working—but my legs weren't," he said. "'I need a break,' I told my guide, then promptly fell down and went to sleep. A half hour later he nudged me, saying it was time to go. After four more hours of stumbling and staggering down the mountain, the guide admitted we might be turned around.

"'What?' I screamed, ready to kill him. 'Now you tell me we're lost?'

Larry Kelly's "piece of cake" sheep was taken after some very hard hunting. He used a Magna-ported T/C Contender in 6.5 JDJ chambering to take the animal at two hundred yards.

"'Not actually lost,' he stammered. 'It's just that everything looks different in the dark.'

"A hard quarter-mile later we were still staring into inky blackness. I couldn't even make out Duane standing next to me. All I could think of was Jim, sleeping soundly in the tent.

"'I think we're getting close,' Duane said after another twenty minutes of walking. At that point I began whistling and shouting, hoping Jim could hear me.

"Miracle of miracles, he finally did, responding with a whistle of his own. I was so happy to hear his whistle I didn't even want to kill him any more. At least not 'til he grinned as I stumbled through the tent door — then said, 'What did I tell you, Kel? Piece of cake!'"

GREAT HUNTS WITH DWIGHT VAN BRUNT

When it comes to hunting, Dwight Van Brunt is a lot more serious than most other handgunners I know. His full-time job as vice president of marketing and sales for Kimber keeps him in constant touch with many people in the shooting industry. That includes outfitters, guides, and other hunters who prefer to use a handgun.

While he's a dedicated 1911 fan, Dwight Van Brunt does much of his handgun hunting with a Freedom Arms .454 Casull revolver with a 7½-inch barrel. A 4-port Mag-na-port has been installed in the barrel. The gun has worn both 2X Leupold and 1.5–4X Burris pistol scopes. "When I do my job, this pistol will easily put five shots into 1.5 minute of angle," he said. "I do my own handloading with Freedom Arms 260-grain JFP bullets."

The first animal Van Brunt took with a handgun was a 9¼-inch billy killed in the mountains just north of Yellowstone Park. The mountain goat was a great start to his hunting career, as it tied the handgun world record.

"After a careful stalk, I surprised the goat napping high on a hillside," Van Brunt said. "He flushed like a quail, and I took him at sixty yards. He was running broadside to me, and I shot him four times. All the bullets passed completely through the animal. He ran right to the edge of a cliff, and luckily collapsed backward into an avalanche chute. If he'd fallen forward, he would have plummeted five hundred feet into a mountain lake."

Two years later, he killed a trophy-class Shiras moose with the same Freedom Arms .454 Casull revolver.

"I was hunting in September near Deer Lodge, Montana," Van Brunt said. "I knew a big bull was in the area, so I hunted hard for several days. I didn't want just *any* moose when there was

Dwight Van Brunt killed this mountain goat in southern Montana with a sixty-yard running shot from his Freedom Arms .454 Casull revolver after a five-hour climbing stalk. The animal tied the existing SCI handgun record. Photo courtesy of Dwight Van Brunt.

Van Brunt was able to call this moose to within sixteen yards before dispatching it with a handgun. Photo courtesy of Dwight Van Brunt.

This SCI Handgun World-Record black bear was killed with a .454 Casull revolver. It squared seven feet. Photo courtesy of Dwight Van Brunt.

a good chance of getting a real trophy. It was hard, frustrating work. Moose are so large you think they'd be easy to find, but they seem to have a way of disappearing when being hunted.

"One morning I finally spotted him. I saw him at a distance, tending a cow. After a long stalk, during which I kept carefully out of sight, I got close enough to try calling. Using only my voice, I got the bull's attention. A few more calls and he headed in my direction. He was just sixteen yards away when I shot him. This was the first moose taken with a pistol that was large enough to qualify for the SCI (Safari Club International) record book.

In 1993, Van Brunt killed an outstanding black bear with his .454 Casull.

"A friend and I trailed this bear for three straight days," Van Brunt recalled. "We were using hounds to track the scent. The hunt took place in May near Coeur d'Alene, Idaho.

"We finally caught up with him at the bottom of a deep canyon," he added. "Centering him in the crosshairs, I fired four times. We later learned one shot was all that was necessary. Each bullet passed all the way through the animal, exiting on the far side.

"The bear was a real monster," Van Brunt said. "After we tanned his hide, it squared seven feet on the nose. It was the handgun world record then—still is, as far as I know."

Chapter 12

HANDGUNS ON SAFARI

AFRICA'S DANGEROUS SEVEN
WITH LYNN THOMPSON

Few hunters have attempted the feat of taking Africa's fabled "Dangerous Seven" with a handgun of any kind. Knifemaker Lynn Thompson succeeded in doing this—not with a scoped, single-shot pistol chambering high-powered rifle cartridges, but with iron-sighted revolvers. Killing big game with a revolver required him to patiently stalk within sixgun range—often only a handful of yards—then rely on unusually high handgunning skills for clean kills. In addition to outstanding marksmanship with an open-sighted revolver, he had to exhibit nerves of cold steel.

CROCODILE

"This ten-foot-plus crocodile was taken in Mozambique on the Zambezi River about twenty miles below Tete," said Lynn Thompson, president of Cold Steel, Inc. "I first spotting him basking in the sun on a small island. We circled behind him, beached the boat, and I began sneaking up on him.

"I'd already shot a 13½-foot crocodile in Tanzania with a rifle, and I hoped to shoot an even bigger one in Mozambique," he added. "However, I had only one day to hunt and was looking to shoot any decent croc I could find. I needed to kill a crocodile with a handgun to complete the Dangerous Seven. Very few countries in Africa will allow you to legally hunt with a handgun. Those I know of include South Africa, Tanzania, Mozambique, and Benin. There may be more, but I'm not aware of them.

"When I finally got close enough to shoot, I was so excited that my first shot went right over the top of him," Thompson pointed out. "I was aiming for the brain located near the end of the crocodile's 'smile.' The range was approximately forty-five yards, which was as close as I could get. I was shooting offhand.

"By the grace of God my second shot—quickly fired double action—struck the crocodile in the head between the snout and his eyes. The hole in his head kept him from submerging, so he had to swim on the surface. Watching carefully, I soon saw him crawl out on a small island about 130 yards away.

"God has blessed me with terrific 20/10 eyesight. When my guide Jeremy insisted what I was looking at was just a beached log, I told him I was sure it was my croc lying there," said Thomp-

This ten-plus-foot crocodile was shot in the Zambezi River by Lynn Thompson. He used a .454 Casull double-action Ruger revolver with iron sights. Photo courtesy of Lynn Thompson.

son. "When I finally got him to look through his binoculars, he said, 'Wow, you're right!'

"We quickly made our way back to our twelve-foot wooden boat, got the twenty-five-horsepower motor fired up and sped toward our quarry," he continued. "When we were forty yards away, my game scout took the oars as Jeremy cut the engine and held the boat steady. Here's where all my practice firing the .454 Casull double action paid off. All three of my shots struck the crocodile, anchoring him for good.

"I am extremely grateful to Ruger for offering the Super Redhawk in .454 Casull chambering—and for the action job performed by Hamilton Bowen," Thompson said. "I have a matching pair of these revolvers with 7½-inch barrels, and they're fantastic firearms. I wouldn't hesitate to take on any animal on earth with these big double-action revolvers."

RHINO

"We began my hunt for rhino early in the morning—about 6:00 AM," Thompson said. "My P.H. (Professional Hunter) had a pretty good idea where a particular rhino could be found at this time of day, so we set out. After an hour of looking, we came upon him in a meadow. He was about sixty yards away, standing broadside to me. I wanted to take the shot, but the P.H. insisted we could get in closer. As we tried to move up, the rhino took off at a trot. It was two hours later before we saw him again.

"My next opportunity to shoot was even less desirable," Lynn recalled. "The rhino was partially obscured by thick bushes, and stood quartering away from me. The range was over one hundred yards. I tried to angle my shot into the chest, but succeeded in only breaking a shoulder. Away he went, knocking down small trees and busting through heavy brush like it wasn't even there. We took up the spoor and had seven more hours of

As part of his Big Five/Dangerous Seven collection, Thompson shot this SCI Gold Medal rhino with a .454 Casull revolver. The first shot was at one hundred yards, the second at twenty yards.

hard walking ahead before we came up on him again. By now he was in a pretty bad way. I was able to move up to within twenty yards, then put a round into the brain to finish him. I was using my 7½-inch-barreled Freedom Arms .454 Casull with iron sights, and shooting Cor-Bon's excellent 360-grain FMJ Penetrators.

"My rhino scored very high in the SCI record book. I believe he's number twenty-two in the overall category, which is pretty good when you consider he was shot with an iron-sighted handgun. The hunt took place near Hoedspruit, South Africa. As usual, my primary P.H. was Harry Claassens, who has accompanied me on all nine of my African safaris."

LEOPARD

"My memorable leopard hunt took place in Tanzania's Selous Game Reserve in 1999," Thompson remembered. "After doing my best to remain motionless in a cramped, airless blind for six hours a day, fifteen days straight, I was tired, miserable, and discouraged. It was the most difficult hunt I'd ever attempted.

"The blind overlooked a tree that should have been irresistible to a hungry leopard, particularly since Harry Claassens had baited it with an impala ram I'd shot the day before. By now the dead impala stank to high heaven, sending a 'come-hither' scent to any big cats in the neighborhood.

"If a leopard showed, I wanted to be within twenty-five yards to be certain of making the shot," Thompson said. "I was using my Freedom Arms .454 Casull revolver, which was equipped with iron sights. Positioning the blind that close to the bait made it extremely difficult to get a leopard to come in. These cats can hear even the smallest noise. To make matters worse, we were so close we were well inside his defensive circle, making the leopard extra wary and easily spooked.

"Early on the sixteenth day, the leopard put in an appearance, climbing the tree at dawn," Thompson recalled. "Standing over the bait, he gave me a broadside shot. I distinctly remember aiming just behind his shoulder, and having a rock-solid sight picture as I touched off the three-pound trigger. At the shot, the cat leapt from the tree without making a sound. He gave no visible sign of being hit.

"We waited fifteen minutes, then approached the tree to look for sign. A careful search didn't turn up a single drop of blood. Searching wider yielded similarly sobering results. After a still wider search of half an hour, Guy Rowe and Harry Claassens, my P.H.s, were both convinced I'd missed.

"'I *couldn't* have missed,' I insisted. 'The shot was perfect!'

"We decided to make one last try, and cut an even wider loop looking for spoor of the wounded cat. After ten minutes of looking, one of the game scouts shouted, 'Blood!' All at once, our hearts began to thunder. 'Great,' I thought, 'a wounded leopard to follow with no idea where or how badly he was hit.'

"Harry was carrying his beloved CZ .375 H&H Magnum, which he'd had customized over many years until it suited him perfectly. Guy Rowe was carrying a .458 Winchester Magnum over-and-under double rifle, also made by CZ. In 2001, he'd used the rifle to shoot a charging leopard through the eye at point-blank range. The leopard had begun his charge from just seven yards away!

"I was carrying the only weapon I had with me, my single-action .454," Thompson said. "I'll never forget Harry's words: 'Now don't let your guard down, Lynn. It's up to you to stop this leopard. Don't depend on Guy or myself to hit him, because we can easily miss. Be sure you're prepared to stop him by yourself.' At these words, my hair really stood on end.

Thompson spent more than fifteen straight days in a blind in pursuit of this leopard. Photo courtesy of Lynn Thompson.

"We took up the spoor," Thompson continued. "At first, the trail took us through fairly thin brush—but after one hundred yards or so it led into the thick stuff, and our pace slowed to a crawl. We painstakingly scrutinized literally every scrap of brush and every bush for a hiding leopard preparing to charge.

"Slowly, we moved into even thicker foliage, then Harry shouted, 'Here he is!' I'll tell you my heart jumped in my throat as I made my way to where Harry was pointing to my leopard. The big cat was on his side, dead as a mackerel. He was in a small undercut on the side of a brush-choked ravine. The leopard weighed 140 pounds, about average for a mature, full-grown leopard in that part of Tanzania.

"My first and only shot had taken him through the lungs, the 300-grain JSP punching through both sides of the animal. In retrospect, I wished I'd used a 260-grain JHP. However, at the time I didn't want to have to change my sight setting to accommodate the lighter load."

CAPE BUFFALO

"In 1999, we began our buffalo hunt in Tanzania's Selous Game Reserve by getting up before daylight and driving dirt roads in the area looking for some sign that a buffalo herd passed during the night," said Thompson. "A half hour later, we came to a spot where the road had been chopped up by big herd that'd recently crossed. We took up their spoor and gave chase.

"It was pretty easy going at first, but by the time we caught up with the herd six hours later, the grass was over my head. I'm 5 feet, 9 inches tall, which meant the grass was more than six feet high. As we moved through the tall grass, we met up with the rear of the herd and spotted a big lone bull bringing up the rear. Since I had only a couple of days left in my twenty-one-day hunt, we decided to try and take him. We carefully moved up so I could get a broadside shot.

"We approached to within forty yards, and it was apparent we couldn't stalk any closer," Thompson said. "The bull had changed position, and was now facing us head-on. This is my least favorite position for taking any animal, let alone a Cape buffalo, but I decided to take the shot. I nestled the front sight in the middle of his chest and tripped the trigger. The trigger pull on my matched set of Freedom Arms .454 Casulls must be experienced to be believed. The letoff is exceptionally crisp and easy to control.

"At the shot, the bull whirled into the grass, but we all agreed he was hard hit. We waited the customary ten or fifteen minutes for him to 'stiffen up,' then we took up the spoor. There was no shortage of blood, and we stayed on the spoor for another twenty minutes before we found him standing under a tree. He was obviously in a bad way, but it took three more shots at approximately thirty-five yards to put him down. I remember cocking that single action as fast as I could. We'd already walked for many hours, and I didn't feel like chasing a wounded buffalo until dark.

This buffalo was killed in high grass at the Selous Game Reserve in Tanzania. It was one of three Thompson took with a .454 Casull revolver.

"When he hit the ground, we all thought he was dead," said Thompson. "But I still approached very gingerly as I moved in close for the final finisher. With buffalo, it pays to make sure. We were just eight feet away when he lurched to his feet. It was one of those heart-stopping moments you read about but seldom encounter. However, I was ready and shot him one last time through the neck. The bullet exited through his right eye, putting him down for the count. It all happened so fast that neither P.H. could get a rifle up. This proved to me that, up real close, a handgun is far faster than any rifle."

LION

"I'd been trying to get within good handgun range of a male lion with a nice mane, but after two weeks of hard hunting in Mozambique, I settled for a big female," said Thompson. "The revolver I was using—a double-action Ruger Super Redhawk in .454 Casull—weighed fifty-four ounces. I carried it on my right side in a black Cordura hip holster made by Uncle Mike's. This holster has been used almost continuously since 1989. It was designed for a gun with a nine-inch barrel, but I liked it because it swallowed up a large-frame revolver with a 7½-inch barrel, completely encasing the rear sights and trigger guard, while leaving the butt sticking out. It was a little slow on the draw, but gave great protection to the revolver and retained it securely without the need for a safety strap.

"She and another lioness came into the bait (a large bullock) we'd anchored to a huge log on the edge of a dry river bottom. It was nearly 5:30 in the afternoon, and we'd been suffering in the blind's blistering heat for the past several hours," Thompson recalled. "At first the big lioness sniffed around the bait, but she heard some monkeys chattering nearby and moved off. A few minutes later we heard one hell of a commotion—then silence, followed by the

After two weeks of hunting, Lynn Thompson killed this big female lion at thirty yards with his double-action Ruger .454 Casull.

sound of crunching bones as she noisily consumed the monkey she'd killed. After finishing this snack, she returned to the bait.

"Wasting no more time, I smacked her on the shoulder from about thirty yards. She fell over, then went into a roll as my second shot—fired double action—went slightly high, just over her back. I continued firing double action as quickly as I could. My third and fourth shots hit her hard, laying her low. Then I ran up very close and gave her the rest of the cylinder just to make sure.

"She was a very large lioness, weighing over three hundred pounds and well into her prime," he said. "I was using Winchester 300-grain JSP .454 Casull ammunition, which chronographs from my Super Redhawk's 7½-inch barrel at over 1,600 fps. For me, this is a very controllable load in a fifty-four-ounce revolver. At fifty yards, I can consistently keep all my double-action shots (fired roughly 1½ seconds apart) in a six-inch circle.

"To prepare for this hunt, I fired more than 2,000 rounds of PMC and Black Hills .357 magnum rounds double action, 1,000 rounds of PMC .44 magnum, and 600 rounds of Winchester's 300-grain JSP .454 Casull factory loads."

HIPPOPOTAMUS

"I believe my SCI Gold Medal hippopotamus is the third largest ever taken with a handgun," Lynn Thompson said. "It's also the third hippopotamus I've killed with my single-action .454 Casull revolver. I used Cor-Bon ammunition loaded with 335-grain hard-cast lead bullets.

"The hunt took place in 1999 in the Selous Game Reserve of Tanzania. One of my P.H.s, Guy Rowe, had spotted this big bull on a hunt three weeks earlier, so after I collected my leopard we thought we'd give him a go. After a 4:00 AM start, we traveled two hours from camp, hoping to catch the bull on the riverbank as it was returning from feeding all night in the forest.

"As luck would have it, we were too late. The hippo had already returned to the river and joined his cows. Glassing carefully, we finally found him several hundred yards away. Trouble was, we couldn't find an approach route that would get me into

Thompson killed this SCI Gold Medal hippo with one shot to the brain at twenty-five yards. Recovering the dead animal from the river was dangerous work.

good handgun range. We finally decided the only thing to do was to crawl on our hands and knees, and finally our bellies, to get to a small, rocky outcropping from which I could shoot. I hate to get dirty, but love to hunt—so I crawled across the sand, rocks, sticks, and other debris on the riverbank, keeping as low a profile as possible. The stalk took twenty minutes, but I finally managed to get into a good prone position about twenty-five yards away.

"I eased back the hammer of my Freedom Arms .454 and heard a gritty noise that made me cringe. Sand had obviously gotten into the action, but I had a good rest and a rock-solid sight picture. I needed to hit a target just two inches wide and four inches high to put the bullet into the brain box. I waited for the perfect opportunity, then let fly.

As I brought the big gun down out of recoil, I heard Guy Rowe say, 'A perfect brain shot!' Harry Claassens, my other P.H., then brought up the video camera and played the action back. We could all see the shot had gone true. We knew the hippopotamus was dead, but it'd disappeared under the water.

"Now came the moment we all dreaded," Thompson recalled. "The Rufiji's current moved pretty fast and we didn't want to lose him—but we were all nervous about the big crocodiles we'd seen the previous day less than a hundred yards off.

"Lacking a boat or canoe, we decided to wade for him. Poles were cut, then Guy and Harry waded up to their armpits into the river, as I fired into the water around them. We hoped this would scare off any hungry crocodiles lurking just out of sight. After several anxious minutes spent probing the river bottom, we located the hippo and tied a stout rope to one hind leg. The rope was then attached to the winch on the Toyota truck, which laboriously pulled the animal out on dry land.

"After field dressing and skinning the hippo, we split the carcass into quarters to use for lion bait," Thompson said. "Then we loaded the meat and hide into our only truck. The problem was that the riverbank was so high we couldn't drive the overloaded truck up it. After several scary attempts to muscle our way up, we decided there was no help for it and spent two and a half hours digging and hacking a path to make it possible for the Toyota to trundle up the steep bank and return to the trailhead."

ELEPHANT

"I was hunting on a ranch next to the Klasserie Game Reserve near Hoedspruit, South Africa," Thompson recalled, "when my P.H. Harry Claassens and I ran across a rogue elephant that had escaped the reserve and was being very destructive to the vegetation and animals on the neighboring private lands.

"This big bull was bad news for everyone," he said. "The game department had made several attempts to drive him back onto the reserve, but he wouldn't stay there. He merely pushed the fences over and went on his merry way. The area was experiencing a severe drought, and resources were very scarce. All the animals were in poor condition, and this elephant was determined to find greener pastures. Competition for food was so severe we even videotaped this bull attacking a big bull rhino to drive him away from a feeding spot.

"I admit I have strong reservations about shooting elephants, as I admire them very much," Thompson said. "But after being assured the game department was going to shoot him if I didn't, I agreed to the hunt. Once I paid several thousand dollars in conservation fees, the hunt was on.

"The next morning, we approached the area where the elephant had been last seen, and soon came upon him. He was totally unafraid of us, standing his ground until we were twenty yards away. This was too close. He took a few steps and shook his head, trumpeting his annoyance.

"I'd intended to go for the brain shot, but that's an awfully small target when you're using a revolver with iron sights," Thompson remembered. "The elephant was twisting his huge body back and forth and shaking his head. I was afraid of missing the brain and just pissing him off. Too, my wife was videotaping the action, and I'd promised her mother I wouldn't get her killed.

"I decided to take the much safer and surer lung shot. As he turned broadside, I shot him on the shoulder with my Freedom Arms .454 Casull. At the shot, he turned and ran straight away from me. I quickly put a round through both hips from the rear. The effects of these shots turned him, showing me his uninjured side, and I put another bullet through his lungs before he lumbered out of sight.

"Now I was good and scared," Thompson said. "I'd fired all but one of my 360-grain Cor-Bon FMJ Penetrators, and all I had left for follow-ups was 300-grain JSP ammo. Since I possessed the heaviest rifle, I gave my custom .416 Remington (Randy Brooks

This rogue bull took four 350-grain Cor-Bon solids from a .454 Casull before going down. Professional Hunter Harry Claassens is at left, Lynn Thompson at right.

of Barnes Bullets made it for me on a 1909 Mauser Action) to Harry and we set off.

"It was all I could do to put one foot in front of the other. I didn't know if those 300-grain JSP bullets would penetrate through to an elephant's brain if I had to stop a charge with a frontal shot. But I couldn't let Harry go by himself, so I forced myself to run up in front of Harry and join him in taking up the spoor.

"After twenty minutes of tracking, we found the bull crumbled up dead in an unusual kneeling position," he said. "The ivory weighed approximately thirty-five to thirty-eight pounds a side.

"We spent all morning skinning and crudely butchering the beast," Thompson recalled. "Later, we saw that the meat was distributed to more than forty families who were badly in need of the protein. They were overjoyed at this windfall of tasty meat."

In addition to taking Africa's Dangerous Seven with an iron-sighted revolver, Lynn Thompson has handgunned numerous other African trophies. To mention only a few, these kills include a large wildebeest that required six shots from his Freedom Arms .454 Casull. Thompson's first shot from offhand at ninety-four yards struck the animal's chest, critically wounding it. However, it took five more rounds to bring this incredibly tough animal down to stay.

Thompson also shot a good warthog with the same gun, again offhand at almost identical range. Cor-Bon's 300-grain jacketed softpoint ammo was used. Earlier he shot an impala off-hand at sixty yards—yet again with the same gun and load. The only round he fired took the animal through the heart.

Not all of Thompson's kills were made with bigbore revolvers, though. He killed another impala by shooting it in the neck with a .22 Winchester Rimfire Magnum single-action Freedom Arms revolver. The range was fifty yards.

TED NUGENT ON THE DARK CONTINENT

Here's Nuge's story about an African handgun hunting adventure, written in his own inimitable style.

Each daybreak stroll along the Blydes River deep within the South African bush brought my family and me great calm and peace. Birds of every description emerged from the riverine habitat, bringing beautiful, awakening songs to the sub-Saharan scrub. All sunrises and sunsets are special no matter where you find them, but something powerful glows and grows across the soul and landscape with each incremental warming inch of fiery sunlight, basting the African veldt around you. It's more orange than gold, with just a touch of pink on the rock formations at river's edge. The wind is always gentle at this time, and my step seems more relaxed and slower, yet more alive than usual. It's good for me.

A little later this morning, I would head for the Hoedspruit Airport in south-central South Africa for our re-

This African impala fell to Ted Nugent's 10mm Glock, proving that auto pistols do have a place in the hunting field.

Ted Nugent also killed this warthog with a 10mm Glock pistol.

turn home to America after another wonderful African safari with family and friends. The archery cases and luggage were locked up and loaded in the "combi" for the short ride, but I craved one last goodbye walk to watch and hear the behemoth hippos raise white-water hell in the pools at the bend down-river from camp.

As usual, for commonsense, self-defense reasons, I wore my Glock M20 in a Galco strongside hip holster loaded with sixteen rounds of 135-grain Cor-Bon, bonded jacketed hollow-points, with my ever-ready double spare magazine pouch carrying the extra thirty rounds. Hell, you'd think I was going to Detroit.

One's spirit and mind work amazingly efficiently under these inspiring conditions, and as I walked I sensed a tiny movement far off in the thornscrub to my left.

Very slowly I raised my small Leupold binoculars to identify a large, gray warthog rubbing his fanny against a small tree. I estimated him to be about one hundred yards away through sparse grasses and brush, and I filled my hand with the Mag-na-ported Glock 10mm in a single, smooth, slow-motion draw. The 250-

pound porker paused and looked north as the Trijicon three-dot sight settled on his forward torso, and the slight creep of the 3½-pound Glock trigger came back like it had thousands and thousands of times at the range. I breathed deep, let it out about halfway, and the gun went off.

Instantaneously, the *whomp* of the bullet came back to my ears and the beast tipped over in a swirl of dust and kicking feet. I counted 106 paces to the now-motionless boar and examined the small hole on his right side, as well as the massive, bloody wound exiting his left shoulder. It was as if I had nailed him with a full-house .30–06 deer load. The kinetic energy produced at 1,450 feet per second by this superior cartridge is testament to the power and efficiency of good handgun caliber loadings designed specifically for big game hunting and self-defense.

He was stunning in his ugly beastliness, with good six-inch ivory tusks protruding from the nasty prehistoric porcine lips on his wart-riddled face. Warthogs are so ugly that they are beautiful. And the meat is fantastic. This night an entire village of natives would dine like kings, compliments of the team of the Great Spirit, Cor-Bon, Glock, and Hunka Ted.

HANDGUNNING ELEPHANT WITH LARRY KELLY

"It was my ninth hunt for elephant," Larry Kelly said. "So far, I'd taken five bulls with a rifle and four with a handgun—all with shots to the brain. This time I had a problem. Concerned with breaking the animal's tusks if he collapsed on the rocky ground, which seemed to be everywhere, my P.H. Don Price wanted me to shoot for the chest.

"Any elephant hunter knows you can't drop one in its tracks with a lung shot. If the bull didn't go down immediately, I knew Don would be backing me up with his .458. But I didn't want any-

It takes skill and nerve to tackle an elephant with a handgun. Photo courtesy of Larry Kelly.

one else putting bullets into my elephant—and I didn't want to track a wounded bull for a couple of days to finish him off.

"I carried two revolvers, including my Stalker—a Ruger Super Blackhawk wearing a 2X Leupold scope and an 8⅜-inch Magna-ported barrel," Kelly said. "My other gun was a single-action Ruger Predator, an open-sighted sixgun carried in my belt holster. Both guns were stoked with .44 magnum ammo loaded with sturdy 320-grain bullets produced by SSK and Ohio Shooter's Supply.

"After days of hard hunting, we had headed to a nearby area where a couple of bulls had just been reported. Arriving at daybreak, I'd followed Don and two native trackers into the bush. Within an hour, we'd heard the distinctive, branch-cracking sound of elephants feeding. One tracker kept back, while Don, the other tracker, and I had circled downwind to begin our stalk.

"Suddenly Don and Teteu, the tracker, stooped low and stopped, motioning me to do the same," Kelly recalled. "After a

moment of searching the brush ahead, I finally made out a feeding bull just thirty-five yards away. The bull was on a rise above us, head and tusks visible on the skyline.

"'He'll go maybe sixty pounds,' Don hissed. 'Take him!'

"Drawing the hammer back, I decided to try for the brain," Kelly said. "I thought that was the surer shot to take, particularly with my .44 magnum. As soon as I took aim, Don poked me in the chest and whispered, 'Shoot him in the heart!'

"I placed the crosshairs where I thought the heart would be and pulled the trigger. The bull let out a chilling roar and threw up his massive head. I quickly sent a second round on its way, again aimed for the heart. The animal turned and vanished from sight.

"We heard the bull crashing through the brush, then silence," Kelly recalled. "The animal had run only twenty yards before going down. We cautiously approached together, Don with his rifle up and ready.

"'Don't get in front of him,' Don shouted.

"From a couple of yards away, I fired a finishing shot at the bull's head," Kelly said. "The range was too close for the scope, so the bullet didn't go where intended. I finally unholstered my iron-sighted, 4⅜-inch .44 magnum Predator and put a 320-grain bullet into the animal's brain."

J. D. JONES, HANDGUNNING PIONEER

J. D. Jones is another famous handgunner who has hunted throughout the world—including Africa on countless occasions. Founder and owner of SSK Industries, Jones made an important contribution to handgun hunting by developing his famous "Hand Cannons." Using the Thompson/Center Contender or Encore pistols as a platform, these long-barreled single shots are chambered for the huge number of JDJ cartridges Jones has developed over the years. Designed specifically for Jones's beefed-up barrels, these cartridges take hunting handgun performance to a whole new level.

J. D. Jones killed this magnificent kudu with a handgun.

Jones is the founder of Handgun Hunters International (H.H.I.), an organization devoted specifically to promoting the sport of handgun hunting. Members receive up-to-date information about guides and outfitters and the success (or lack of success) handgunners have experienced with them. Other benefits include the opportunity to purchase hunting equipment at discounted prices and participate in H.H.I. big game and varmint hunts. Not incidentally, members also receive extensive hunting handgun reloading data.

A much-published writer of handgun hunting books and articles, Jones is also publisher and editor of *The Sixgunner* magazine. One of the most experienced—if not the most experienced—of those who've hunted Africa with a handgun, he deserves mention here. He has been voted Handgun Hunter of the Year, and has received the prestigious Outstanding American Handgunner Award.

Chapter 13

CUSTOMIZED HUNTING HANDGUNS

M any gunsmiths install aftermarket parts and add other custom touches to handguns. The majority of this work has been done on .45 ACP 1911 auto pistols and other guns intended for self-defense. Competitive shooters are also regular customers of custom gunsmiths.

When it comes to customizing hunting handguns, two names top the list.

Larry Kelly, founder of Mag-na-port International, Inc., and J. D. Jones of SSK Industries helped pioneer handgun hunting. In addition to breaking ground that made hunting with a handgun the increasingly popular and widely recognized sport it is today, they were the first to modify handguns specifically to improve their performance in the hunting field.

MAG-NA-PORT INTERNATIONAL, INC.

When Larry Kelly first began hunting with a handgun, he found that the recoil and muzzle jump from his .44 magnum Ruger

Blackhawk affected accuracy and made it difficult to fire a quick, aimed follow-up shot.

Kelly had gained specialized experience with Electrical Discharge Machining (EDM) while working on fuel control valves for spacecraft on the Apollo project. By 1965, he developed the concept of cutting trapezoidal ports into a handgun muzzle using EDM.

In 1969, Apollo EDM was formed, with only a small part of the new company's business related to firearms. Soon, firearms writers began paying attention to how handguns customized by Kelly performed. His muzzle-porting process proved so effective that it created a growing demand for this work. By 1973, Kelly had sold his interest in Apollo EDM and was performing this work on handguns on a full-time basis.

The Mag-na-port shop first operated as part of a small retail store in Fraser, Michigan. Mag-na-port has since ported tens of

Mag-na-port International's custom Stalker .44 magnum.

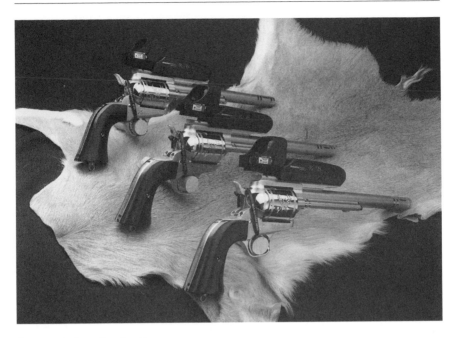

Custom single-action hunting guns.

thousands of firearms, ranging from .22LR target pistols to .460 Weatherby Magnums. In 1983 Mag-na-port Arms, Inc., with additional franchises in Australia and New Zealand, became Mag-na-port International, Inc., and moved into a larger plant in Harrison Township, Michigan.

Mag-na-porting is a surgically precise method of removing metal using the EDM process. Dielectric oil is flooded over the area of barrel to be ported, and an electrode is moved into position. Applying voltage ionizes the oil and establishes a flow of electrons (an electrical arc) between electrodes and barrel. The trapezoidal ports are "machined" by the electron flow.

The patented Mag-na-port process creates a smooth incision of exact dimension. The metal surrounding the ports receives no damage or machining marks. The gun's finish is also unchanged.

It's blended into the metal exposed by the erosion process during the EDM operation.

The company notes that Mag-na-porting doesn't reduce bullet velocity or affect a gun's accuracy. And unlike conventional porting or muzzle brakes, it doesn't increase noise levels. However, it does reduce muzzle lift and perceived recoil.

Handgun recoil—more specifically, felt recoil—affects individual shooters differently. Less experienced shooters will be more aware of the reduction of felt recoil in a gun that has been Mag-na-ported. The degree of change in a handgun's shooting characteristics after Mag-na-porting depends upon many factors: barrel length, weight, and most critically, the ammo with which the gun is loaded.

Traditional Mag-na-porting consists of two trapezoidal ports cut into a handgun's barrel approximately half an inch from the muzzle. These ports are placed at an angle of approximately thirty-five to forty-five degrees. This translates into a fifteen to twenty percent reduction in perceived recoil.

Two trapezoidal ports and two oval ports cut into the sides of the barrel is a style of Mag-na-porting available on barrels of 7½ inches or longer. It's recommended for hunting handguns, particularly larger calibers. The side ports provide additional reduction in recoil and aid barrel stability.

Dual trapezoidal Mag-na-porting is designed for guns with shorter barrels (three-inch minimum barrel length). On defensive or concealed-carry handguns, this style of porting is highly effective in reducing muzzle lift.

The Mag-na-port process itself doesn't change a handgun's accuracy. The improvement comes from the fact that the gun is more comfortable to shoot. Because of its softer recoil, the gun can also be returned to firing position more quickly.

A Mag-na-ported, heavily customized Ruger Super Blackhawk.

A Smith & Wesson revolver with Mag-na-ported barrel.

Mag-na-port also offers its new Mag-na-brake to further reduce recoil in heavy-kicking magnum handguns. Less than two inches long, the Mag-na-brake is threaded to the muzzle. It has what the company calls "progressive integrated exhaust chambers" that help neutralize the effect of expanding gases. These gases are directed forward at an angle that minimizes sound pressure levels.

This muzzle brake can be installed on round-barreled revolvers like the Ruger Super Redhawk and Super Blackhawks or single-shot pistols like the Thompson/Center Contender. A minimum barrel length of 7½ inches is required for this procedure.

Larry Kelly's Mag-na-porting is widely recognized as one of the most effective ways—probably *the* most effective way—to soften the effect of recoil when shooting high-powered hunting handguns.

SSK INDUSTRIES

J. D. Jones, owner of SSK Industries, has been heavily involved with Thompson/Center Contenders since 1969. He has used these single-shot handguns on all six huntable continents. In addition, he has developed numerous cartridges adapted to Contenders that develop higher power levels without affecting safety and reliability.

The first high-powered load Jones developed for the Contender was the .375 JDJ. It has accounted for more African big game than any other handgun caliber. It's also a fine choice for hunting deer at ranges out to 250 yards. Jones says suitable .375 bullets are available for hunting everything from prairie dogs to elephants. SSK hunting handguns are in use worldwide, with the .375 JDJ widely considered *the* caliber for serious handgun hunting.

This custom SSK Hand Cannon has a cannon-configured barrel.

Diamond-shaped barrels are available from SSK for certain revolvers and Ruger .22 auto pistols.

Jones has devoted a great deal of his life to ballistic research and the development of sporting, law enforcement, and military cartridges and the firearms they chamber.

J. D. began hunting small game when he was thirteen years old. At the same age, he was also taught bullet casting and reloading by a local gunsmith. In the early 1960s, he and Lee Jurras developed the first true high-performance handgun ammunition for revolvers and auto pistols. This was marketed as Super Vel Ammunition, which provided the base that every manufacturer in the world now uses to produce high-performance handgun ammunition.

SSK Industries was founded in 1977 to manufacture and market specific products related to hunting handguns and ammunition. Custom Contender barrels chambered in JDJ calibers

This engraved .375 JDJ Hand Cannon sports an octagon barrel.

specifically designed for hunting soon became the major product of the firm. These precision barrels have a seldom-challenged reputation for delivering a very high degree of accuracy. Mounted on a Contender frame, they give the Thompson/Center pistol truly effective big game harvesting ability.

Early on, Jones decided SSK Industries would manufacture and market only very high quality products. He also made the decision to keep the company small. SSK soon earned a worldwide reputation for manufacturing custom, premium-quality firearms for handgun hunting. In addition to customized Contenders, these products include custom revolvers and bolt-action pistols.

When Thompson/Center Arms introduced its beefier Encore pistol, it created a platform for even more efficient handgun cartridges, which Jones proceeded to develop. Currently, JDJ cartridges based on the old reliable .30–06 rifle case equal or surpass the performance of the belted-magnum-cased cartridges in the Encore.

The more than two hundred cartridges chambered for the Contender include JDJ series rounds in almost every caliber. The most popular are the .226, 6mm, .257, 6.5mm, .270, and 7mm JDJ, which are all based on the very strong .225 Winchester case. For long-range varmint shooting, the .257 JDJ throws an 85-grain bullet at 2,900 fps, and this same load is excellent for hunting pronghorn and whitetail deer. The .309, 8mm, 338 #2, .358, .375, and .416 JDJ cartridges are based on the .444 Marlin case.

The 6.5 JDJ propels 120-grain bullets at 2,400 fps, the .309 uses 165-grain bullets, also at 2,400 fps, while the .375 JDJ starts a 220-grain projectile at 2,250 fps. The same round loaded with 300-grain full-metal-jacketed bullets at 2,000 fps is more than adequate for hunting elephants. In 1984, .375 JDJ handguns were used in nineteen different elephant kills.

Designed for T/C Encore pistols, SSK's 6.5 Mini-Dreadnought (based on the .220 Swift case) develops 2,900 fps with a

SSK Industries offers a wide variety of barrel configurations.

A Flatside .223 Contender with octagon barrel and color case-hardened base and rings.

120-grain bullet. It kills deer at three hundred yards with very little recoil. JDJ rounds are built around modified .30–06 cases and usually produce higher velocities than their equivalent belted-magnum counterparts in the shorter pistol barrels. At the other end of the caliber scale, the .416 JDJ propels a 300-grain bullet at 2,300 fps, and the heavier 400-grain bullet at 2,200 fps. These cartridges are maximized for case capacity and have shortened necks and sixty-degree shoulders.

SSK offers the customized Contender as a complete gun, or high-quality custom "drop in" barrels may be purchased to fit your frame. SSK's standard barrel blank is manufactured by Shilen, whose barrels have won more benchrest matches than any other manufacturer. This accuracy is reflected in SSK custom barrels. If Shilen doesn't offer a particular caliber, SSK turns to another premium barrelmaker to get it. SSK barrel lugs, welding, and heat treating duplicate factory specifications.

Thompson/Center's Encore pistol is exceptionally strong and capable of enormous power. It's larger and at least a pound

An octagon-barreled custom Ruger Super Blackhawk from SSK Industries.

heavier than the Contender. It also usually needs a trigger job to enable the shooter to maximize its inherent accuracy.

The Encore is capable of handling far higher pressures than the Contender. Fired in the Encore, factory .308 Winchester loads produce ballistics approximately equal to the .309 JDJ, but they cannot be chambered in the Contender. SSK barrels designed for the Encore can safely chamber any cartridge with the case head size and pressure level of the .300 Winchester Magnum. The .300 and .338 Winchester mags are fairly popular, as is the .375 H&H.

Increasing the case head size beyond this means you must reduce pressure. Cartridges such as the .470 nitro in factory pressure levels are acceptable to the Encore. The .375 H&H, .416 Taylor (.416/458), and .416/348 JDJ are worth consideration for really big game, and the .500 Alaskan is popular. The .458 Winchester mag is okay, but acceptable only to hardened shooters.

The extra pound of weight in the Encore helps absorb the hard-kicking recoil. Its action is significantly different from that of the Contender. While the Contender sports a better trigger, a good trigger pull can be achieved with the Encore. But if an Encore trigger is adjusted to give an extremely light pull, it may produce ignition and safety problems. There is no significant difference in inherent accuracy between these two T/C pistols.

A significant advantage of the Encore is its ability to handle a large number of factory rifle cartridges that offer high performance without the necessity of reloading. However, significant ballistic advantages are still available to the handloader or wildcatter.

While dozens of other custom gunmakers are available to work on your handgun, Larry Kelly and J. D. Jones have long specialized in improving the performance and handling characteristics of handguns used by serious hunters.

Contact information:
Mag-na-port International, Inc.
41302 Executive Drive
Harrison Township, MI 48045
586-469-6727
www.magnaport.com

SSK Industries
590 Woodvue Lane
Wintersville, OH 43953
740-264-0176
www.sskindustries.com

Chapter 14

CREATING HUNTING HANDLOADS

While economy isn't the main reason for loading hunting handgun ammo, rolling your own can save you money. Handloading allows you to reuse the most expensive component of the ammunition you buy—that costly case.

More important to hunting handgunners, though, is the ability to precisely tailor a load to fit a certain handgun or to meet specific hunting needs. While more and more factory ammo is loaded to hunting parameters, much of the handgun fodder available across the country is designed for plinking or self-defense.

A centerfire handgun cartridge consists of a hollow brass casing, a small cup-shaped primer, powder, and a bullet. When the cartridge is fired, the primer is expended, the powder ignites, and the bullet is propelled from the gun en route to the target, but the case remains in good shape—although slightly expanded. Because the case is by far the most costly part of the cartridge, using it over and over makes good economic sense. Replace the primer, powder, and bullet, and the cartridge is ready to shoot again. If that sounds simple, take heart. It really is.

If you own a .44 magnum sixgun and want insurance against disgruntled bears, you can hot-load some hard-cast bullets for maximum penetration. The same medicine adds serious punch to a .357 magnum revolver. Hard-cast lead loads aren't available at your local sporting-goods store.

By the same token, handgunners can buy premium hunting bullets not offered in factory-loaded fodder from several savvy component manufacturers. These are available in a wide variety of weights, and range from lightly constructed lead-core projectiles suitable for deer or small game to Barnes's all-copper X-Bullets designed for much larger, tougher critters. Comprehensive handloading "recipe books" anyone can follow are available from every major bullet maker. You can push the envelope with max-pressure loads or opt for less velocity and recoil. You're not limited to ammo you'll find on the store shelf.

The only catch is that you first need to buy a reloading outfit and learn how to use it. You must also be willing to set aside an hour or so whenever you need to load up a fresh batch of cartridges.

Reloading inevitably helps you become a better shot for the simple reason that you'll find yourself shooting more often. But more importantly, it makes you a more knowledgeable handgunner and a more effective hunter.

RELOADING TOOLS AND ACCESSORIES

Buying serious reloading equipment can run into money, but complete single-stage outfits are available at surprisingly affordable prices. Still, autoloading, multi-station loading presses can set you back a bundle. The difference between inexpensive and costly outfits can be viewed as a function of the time you're willing to invest to assemble a box of reloads.

Low-priced presses are capable of turning out very fine ammunition, but they're not very speedy. If you intend to do considerable shooting and can't spare a lot of time, these slow, but

A few basic reloading tools, from left: press and dies, powder scale, micrometer.

economical outfits may not be for you. On the other hand, an expenditure of several hundred dollars can't be justified by the amount of handgunning a casual shooter does. Unless money is no object, only a handful of handgun hunters shoot enough to justify buying a progressive, top-of-the-line press. However, the more ammo you build, the more you'll shoot—and you'll need lots of practice to hone your handgunning skills.

Between the two price extremes lies the conventional bench-mounted reloading press. This reasonably priced tool accepts interchangeable screw-in dies to accommodate the full range of handgun (or rifle) cartridges. You also need a powder scale to make sure each propellant charge is accurately weighed (very important!), an inexpensive lubricating pad, and some case lubricant.

While you can get by fine with a bare-bones press, you'll still need a few basic accessories. Most cost only a few dollars or so, and some you can make yourself. For instance, you need some

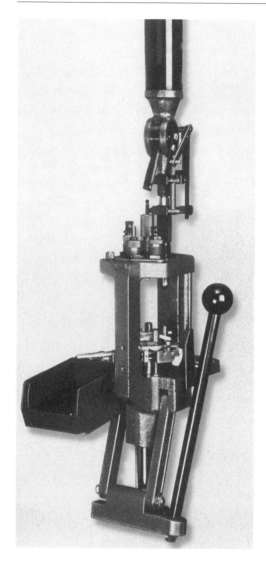

A progressive press speeds up the reloading process.

kind of container or a loading block to hold the cartridge cases upright and close at hand. Once they've been filled with a fresh powder charge, the cases need to be aligned in an orderly fashion for easy inspection. Using a container also lessens the chances of a case being accidentally knocked over, which would result in a powder spill.

A loading block is easy to make if you have access to a drill press. Simply select a drill bit of the proper size (slightly larger in diameter than the base of the cartridge you'll be reloading) and drill several rows of evenly spaced holes in a small block of wood. Set the drill depth so that the bit doesn't completely penetrate the block. Or you can buy a commercial loading block for just a couple of dollars.

Mechanical powder measures automatically throw a measured charge of powder every time the charging handle is cycled.

It's used in conjunction with the powder scale, which is initially used to ensure the measure is properly adjusted to throw the desired amount.

Careful handloaders never depend on mechanical powder measures alone. They'll use one to quickly throw the bulk of the charge—then place the partly loaded cartridge on the scale and trickle the balance of the powder in by hand until the charge is precisely the desired weight. The powder measure speeds up the loading process, but if you're torn between buying a powder measure or a scale, buy the scale. But if you plan to reload more than a few cases at a time, you'll need both.

Other required accessories include a primer pocket brush—an inexpensive little gadget used to clean deposits or debris from primer pockets after the old primer has been removed and before a fresh one is seated. A plastic primer tray is used to orient primers uniformly base-upward where they can be picked up by the primer arm (a tubular tool used to insert fresh primers into

the primer pockets). While the primer arm supplied with many presses speeds up the process, many handloaders prefer to seat primers in a separate operation using more sensitive hand tools.

Finally, be sure to buy at least one good reloading manual with

A series of dies is required to reload handgun cartridges.

recommended loads for the different cartridges you'll be using. This is a must, as there's no room for guesswork at the reloading bench. Handloading reference books are needed to tell you which particular bullet-primer-powder combination is safe in your handgun.

Propellant powders burn at different speeds, so the amount must be carefully varied depending on which powder and bullet weight are used. The wrong combination can result in dangerously high pressures.

That doesn't mean handloading is dangerous. Far from it. As long as you follow the recommendations in your loading manual, and make sure each step is carefully followed, the homemade ammunition you produce will be as safe as the cartridges you buy over the counter. It's possible to make ammunition equal to or even better than the cartridges you can buy commercially. Improving performance is a goal of every handloader, and it's the big reason so many handgun hunters go this route.

You can tailor your handloads to a specific situation—load down for low-recoil, low-cost practice or develop a special hunting load using a heavy, controlled-expanding bullet. Cost alone isn't the reason most shooters reload.

STEP-BY-STEP RELOADING

CASE PREPARATION

The first step in reloading handgun cartridges is to examine the empty cases you'll be working with. Look carefully for dents, split mouths, or other obvious defects. Once-fired cases are usually in pretty good shape, but as they continue to be reused some casualties will inevitably occur. Be sure to glance inside the case to make sure there's no foreign matter present. Damaged cases should be discarded.

Depriming is the first step in preparing an expended cartridge case for a fresh load.

If you have several different brands or case types on hand, they should be sorted into identical lots. Different manufacturers produce case walls of different thickness, and this affects capacity and performance.

Measure each case to be sure it hasn't expanded beyond the recommended length. If it's too long, trim it to the proper size with a case trimmer.

Next, clean the primer pocket with a primer pocket brush, then make a few turns with a chamfering tool inserted in the case mouth. Chamfering the mouth helps the bullet enter the case and prevents bullet shaving.

Cases should then be wiped clean and lightly lubricated. Rolling the empty cases over a lubricated case-lube pad will do the job, but placing several cases on a piece of cloth and spraying them with lubricant is faster and easier. Special resizing lubricant should always be used, as standard machine oils aren't of the proper viscosity.

Most handgun cartridge loading dies come in a three-die set. The first is the resizing die, which contracts the expanded case to

The primer pocket is then carefully cleaned with a small wire brush.

The inside of the case neck is smoothed and slightly beveled with a chamfering tool.

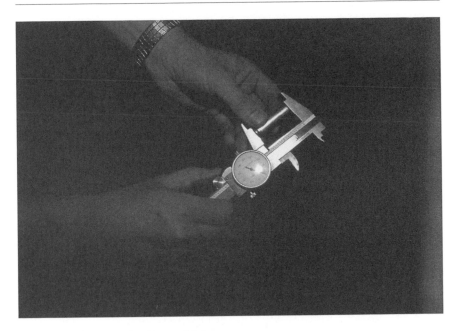

Case length is measured to be sure it's in spec.

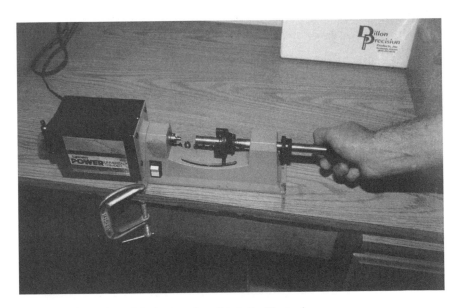

If the case is too long, it's shortened on this lathe-like tool.

a diameter slightly smaller than its original dimensions. A decapping pin incorporated into the die knocks the expended primer from its pocket.

The die should be screwed into the loading press so that the shell holder just contacts the bottom of the die when the press ram (the moving piston under the shell holder) is fully extended. If carbide dies are used, the die should be set slightly higher so there's some clearance between die and shell holder. Otherwise, pressure on the bottom of the die could crack the brittle carbide.

The second die is the expander die. This expands or "bells" the case mouth slightly to more easily accept the bullet. It should be adjusted so that the bullets used will smoothly enter the case mouth. Don't allow too loose a fit or case mouths will split and shorten usable case life.

DECAPPING AND PRIMING

If the decapping operation wasn't performed during resizing, it will be taken care of by the expander die. Once the case has been decapped, smart reloaders use a small, circular wire brush to remove ash or other residue that may remain in the primer pocket. Such deposits can interfere with proper seating of a fresh primer, although some handloaders ignore this step.

Next, a new primer is pressed into the pocket. Take care not to touch the exposed upper section of the primer with oily fingers, as even a small amount of contaminating lubricant can desensitize the explosive compound inside. Sizing lubricant should be wiped from the case surface before re-priming for the same reason.

Many reloading presses feature a priming cup located in the top of the loading ram, or piston, as well as a swinging tube that stores the primers and feeds them one at a time to the cup.

The cup is mounted atop a pivoting arm that swings out of the ram for loading and is then manually pressed back into the

Seating a fresh primer.

ram until it's positioned under the shell holder. The ram is then withdrawn until the primer is seated firmly in the cartridge-case primer pocket. Separate priming tools are available that accomplish this same operation, and many reloaders prefer them.

ADDING POWDER AND BULLETS

Next, powder is loaded into the case. As mentioned earlier, this operation can be quickly performed with a mechanical measure, but topping off a partial load by careful trickling assures greater precision. Before seating a bullet in a loaded case, always look inside the case to make sure it actually contains powder.

The third die is used for bullet seating and crimping, which are performed in the same operation. Most handgun bullets have a crimping groove that shows the proper seating depth. Moving the seating screw in the top of the die adjusts the seating depth, while the body of the die is moved up or down (in its screw

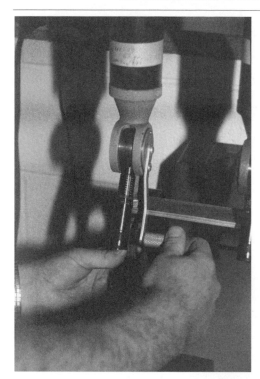

A carefully measured powder charge is added to the primed case.

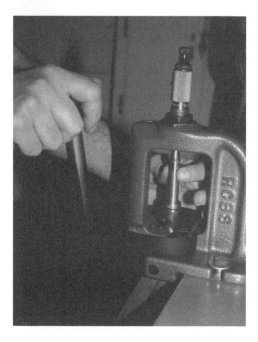

And a new bullet is seated.

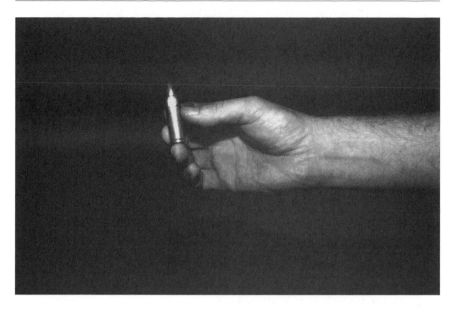

The reloaded round is now ready to use.

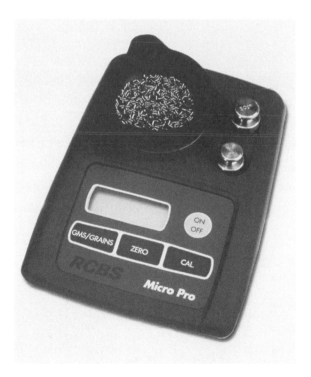

An electronic powder scale is faster and more accurate than a mechanical scale.

mount) to adjust the crimp. Screwing the die body down in the press increases crimp and vice versa.

Light loads need light crimping, while heavy loads using slow-burning powder require a heavier crimp. If the bullets aren't properly crimped, recoil can start them from their cases and then jam the handgun action.

Different loads and bullets are recommended for different purposes. Heavy and/or jacketed bullets moving at high speed are recommended for hunting, while plain lead projectiles at moderate velocities are best for plinking and target work. For deep penetration, hard-cast bullets are sometimes used. Lead bullets should be lubricated to prevent (or at least reduce) lead deposits in the gun's bore.

Almost any centerfire handgun case can be reloaded, but some present fewer problems than others. Revolver cartridges are easy to reload, as they're fed by hand into their individual chambers. Auto-pistol ammunition must be carefully sized to ensure proper feeding. And ammo used in revolvers can be lightly loaded to keep recoil levels down, but auto-pistol cartridges must be loaded to full factory-level pressures or they won't fully cycle the slide. Expended revolver cartridges are obviously easier to retrieve, while auto pistols throw empty brass all over the place.

Large cases are easier to reload than smaller ones are. While .38 Special, .357 magnum, .44 magnum, .44 Special, and .45 ACP cases are easy to work with, smaller hulls present greater difficulties.

RELOADING SAFETY RULES

While reloading is a safe hobby, you must always use common sense. Under no circumstances should you smoke while reloading. Don't drink alcoholic beverages, either. You need a perfectly clear head to avoid potentially dangerous mistakes such as double-charging. Any kind of a spark or open flame could ignite the gunpowder you're working with. If modern smokeless powder does ignite, it won't explode unless tightly contained. Loose powder will rapidly burn with a very hot flame. But water will quench it.

Be particularly careful when handling and storing primers, which are extremely volatile and can be exploded by a sharp blow or jar. They should be stored in the factory containers they came in. Storing loose primers in a glass jar or some similar container is an invitation to disaster. A dropped jar full of primers can become a small bomb with lethal capabilities.

Make sure powders are kept tightly sealed in the containers they came in, and make doubly sure they're not accidentally mixed. Finally, pay careful attention to your loading manual, and don't exceed the maximum charges recommended.

FIELD-TESTING BULLETS AND LOADS FOR SMITH & WESSON'S M500 REVOLVER

The following account by Tim Janzen, director of research and product development for Barnes Bullets, shows how a new bullet for a brand-new handgun was created, carefully handloaded, then tested in the hunting field.

"They're in the clearing on the other side of this bush," my guide Gerrit Nieuwoudt whispered.

We'd been stalking a small herd of twenty blue wildebeest through dense brush for the past half hour, but we still weren't close enough for a good shot with the big revolver I carried. The herd was aware of our presence, though not seriously spooked. On alert, the animals were milling around in the wallows seventy-five yards away. The mature bull I wanted was surrounded by cows.

Gerrit motioned me over to the left side of the bush and whispered, "We'll set up here and hope for a clear shot."

To clear the tall grass in front of me, I'd have to shoot from a sitting position. My Smith & Wesson Model 500 revolver was topped with Burris rings and base and a Burris 2X LER scope. The entire outfit weighed 5 pounds, 10 ounces with a cylinder full of ammo. That's a lot of handgun to hold steady on target for more than a few seconds without some kind of support. I was glad Clair Rees had talked me into taking his Stoney Point shooting sticks along.

The swirling, gusting wind made the crosshairs dance as I looked through the 2X scope. My mounting excitement wasn't helping, either. I leaned forward, hooking my elbows around my knees. Resting the barrel on the crossed shooting sticks, I found a fairly stable shooting position.

Tim Janzen steadies his Burris-scoped .500 S&W revolver on Stoney Point's Steady-Stix.

The bull was facing me head-on, but several cows prevented a clear shot. I quickly ranged the bull with my Leica LRF 800 laser rangefinder. He was eighty-seven yards away—well within the hundred-yard shooting limit I'd set for myself.

Suddenly the bull had had enough. He wheeled and quartered off to the right. Trotting a dozen steps, he cleared the rest of the herd before stopping to look back.

"Take him now," Gerrit said. "If he runs again he'll be out of range."

It wasn't an ideal shot, but would certainly test the performance of the new Barnes 325-grain X-Bullet, just designed for the massive revolver. The bull stood facing away, quartering to the right. The bullet would have to break through the ribs on his right side, travel through the stomach, and penetrate deeply to reach the vitals.

My load was 43.5 grains of H110, ignited by CCI 350 primers. I used Jamison .500 S&W cases, topped off with the new Barnes semi-spitzer, all-copper X-Bullet. The bullets were seated to create an overall cartridge length of 2.275 inches. Case mouths were crimped into the cannelure, with a heavy roll crimp to prevent bullet jump. Muzzle velocity with this load was just over 1,800 fps, producing some 2,350 foot-pounds of muzzle energy.

I'd tested this load in the Barnes Ballistics Lab by shooting through four layers of heavy denim into a block of ten-percent ballistics gelatin. The 325-grain copper bullet produced twenty-three inches of penetration and an awesome wound channel.

Deciding to take the shot, I put the crosshairs on the black animal, trying to line the bullet path up with the far shoulder. As the crosshairs steadied, I applied the final few ounces of trigger pressure and the big gun fired.

As loud as this muzzle-braked gun is—and it *is* loud—all I remember hearing is the *thwack* of the bullet striking. The blue wildebeest staggered, regained its footing, then disappeared into the bush. The rest of the herd followed on the bull's heels.

"Good shot!" Gerrit beamed. "Maybe a bit far back, but he's very sick and will go down soon." We walked to where the bull had been standing when I shot, and immediately spotted blood.

Gerrit runs Constantia Safaris in the northern cape of South Africa and is an excellent P.H. He understood my desire to hunt with the big S&W revolver, and had worked hard to get me within good handgun range. Taking no chances, he turned on his radio and called the main ranch for an experienced tracker to help locate the animal. Wilham, the tracker, arrived twenty minutes later and we set off on the blood trail.

Tim Janzen shot this blue wildebeest with a new Barnes X-Bullet developed for the .500 S&W handgun.

"Be ready," Gerrit ordered. "He might not be dead yet, and could be dangerous in this thick brush."

We lost the trail a few times on the hard, dry ground, but Wilham was amazing. He always managed to find the trail again. After several minutes of searching, Gerrit gave a shout.

The bull was lying dead in the brush only a few hundred yards from where I'd shot. In different terrain, we probably would've seen the animal stagger and fall. Considering the thick brush, credit must be given to Gerrit and Wilham for locating the downed animal so quickly.

When we examined the wildebeest, we found Gerrit had called the shot perfectly. It'd struck some three inches farther back than I'd intended. The bullet broke through the ribs on the bull's right side, ranged through the stomach and up into the vitals, barely catching the corner of the left lung. The bullet broke another rib on the way out. We found it trapped under the skin just behind the left shoulder.

The bullet had functioned perfectly, expanding to 0.97-inch in diameter and retaining one hundred percent of its original weight. It completely penetrated the animal. It was a difficult shot on a tough animal. If I hadn't been sure of what this cartridge and bullet were capable of, I wouldn't have taken the shot. Most bullets would've failed to penetrate to the lungs or would not have expanded to cause the massive trauma and bleeding the 325-grain X-Bullet did.

At the 2003 NRA Show in Orlando, Randy Brooks, owner of Barnes, and I spoke at length with Herb Belin from Smith & Wesson and Peter Pi from Cor-Bon Ammunition about the need for a heavier, long-range X-Bullet for the .500 S&W. Cor-Bon was already loading the Barnes .500-inch, 275-grain XPB bullet. This bullet had received rave reviews because if its excellent accuracy, reduced recoil, and incredible expansion.

But as good as the Barnes 275-grain XPB bullet was, we all recognized that there was room for improvement. Specifically, the relatively light weight of this bullet, combined with its large hollow cavity, result in a low BC (ballistic coefficient) value. A low BC causes the bullet to rapidly shed velocity and energy, limiting its effective range to about one hundred yards.

Cor-Bon's 275-grain XPB ammo is a reduced-pressure, reduced-velocity load suitable for practice and hunting hogs and deer-sized game. Herb and Peter wanted a long-range (200-yard) bullet that would provide the flattest trajectory, maximum kinetic energy, and the legendary Barnes-X terminal performance on large game.

The new bullet was ready within two weeks—an amazing design, engineering, and production feat. Once production samples were available, the bullets were tested by firing them into a deep tank of water at 1,200 and 1,800 fps. They were then fired through four layers of heavy denim (simulating thick animal hide) in front of 8-by-12-inch blocks of calibrated, ten-percent ballistics gelatin. Testing was done at a range of ten feet, with outstanding results.

The wound cavity almost completely gutted the entire first block of gelatin, then tapered off in diameter as it passed through the second block. Total penetration was 23¼ inches. The 325-grain XPB bullet retained one hundred percent of its weight, while expanding to nearly double its original diameter.

During accuracy testing in a return-to-battery machine rest, several five-shot groups were fired at one hundred yards. Accuracy was excellent, hovering right around 1 MOA. Some 300- and 375-grain XPB bullets were also made and tested in the gun. While the heavier 375-grain bullet had a correspondingly higher BC value, it also produced slower velocities when fired at the

Field-testing is important when developing new bullets. This zebra fell to the new 325-grain Barnes X-Bullet.

same pressure. The 325-grain bullet had the edge, with the flattest trajectory and the lowest apparent recoil.

My trip to South Africa had been planned long before we began work on this project. However, the timing worked out perfectly. I received approval from African authorities to take the S&W M500 along on the hunt just days before my departure. With little time to practice, I decided to limit my shooting to a maximum range of one hundred yards. I didn't want to risk losing a wounded animal.

Three days after taking the blue wildebeest, I had the opportunity to shoot a large zebra stallion with the S&W M500 and the new Barnes 325-grain XPB bullet. The distance and angle of the shot were almost identical to what I'd faced with the wildebeest—

as were the final results. Once again the S&W revolver and Barnes bullet were up to the task. The recovered X-Bullet was picture perfect.

Barnes strongly believes in the value of field-testing new products. While laboratory tests gave me confidence in the new bullet and what I could expect it to do to these large, tough animals, testing it in the hunting field provided the ultimate proof of its exceptional performance.

The new .500 S&W 325-grain bullet is available to reloaders from Barnes Bullets, and Cor-Bon will be loading this bullet in its line of .500 S&W ammunition.

Chapter 15

IMPORTANT SAFETY TIPS

Given the proper respect and handled with intelligence, a handgun is as safe as any tool. It's an inanimate object, after all, with no will of its own. Like anything mechanical, it can malfunction—but even a malfunctioning handgun will be perfectly safe if correct handling rules are followed.

If those rules are ignored, however, a handgun can be deadly. Because of its small size and relatively short barrel, the handgun can be more hazardous than rifles and shotguns. It's difficult for the owner of a long-barreled rifle or shotgun to accidentally shoot himself with that firearm. A short-barreled handgun can point almost anywhere in the hands of a careless person—even at the holder.

The handgun is only a recreational tool, but it offers far greater potential for destruction than do most other tools. Improperly handled, it can deal injury and death. If the following "Ten Commandments of Safety" are always observed, you'll never have a shooting accident. (These rules were briefly outlined in chapter 3, but they are so vitally important that they deserve a more detailed discussion.)

TEN COMMANDMENTS OF SAFETY

1. Treat every gun as if it were loaded. All the time. Each and every time you hold it. Most of the other commonsense gun-handling rules are based on this assumption. People are accidentally—and needlessly—killed or wounded every year by "unloaded" guns; that is, the person handling the gun *thought* it was unloaded and treated it carelessly. If you treat every gun you handle—loaded or not—with the proper respect, you'll never have a shooting accident.

2. Watch that muzzle! Never allow the muzzle of your gun to point in any but a safe direction—straight up, at the ground beneath you, or at the target backstop when you're at a shooting range.

3. Never point a gun at anything you don't intend to shoot. And don't touch the trigger until you're *ready* to shoot.

4. Always be sure of your target and backstop. If the bullet misses the target, know where it will go.

5. Whenever you pick up a gun, immediately open the action and inspect for live ammunition. Make sure the action is open (slide locked back on an auto pistol or the cylinder craned open on a double-action revolver) whenever you hand a gun to another person. And if someone hands you a gun with the action closed, open it immediately. Never take someone else's word that a gun is unloaded.

6. Keep guns unloaded when not in use. Never leave the firing range or hunting field, or enter a car or dwelling, with a loaded gun.

7. Be sure the barrel is clear of obstructions before loading or firing. Only check the barrel with the action open and after all the ammunition has been removed.

8. Never shoot at a hard, flat surface or water. When plinking, avoid glass targets. Glass leaves unsightly, dangerous litter and can cause ricochets.

9. Lock and store guns and ammunition separately, out of the reach of children. The best insurance against firearm accidents in the home is a good, locking safe designed specifically for storing guns. Safes also protect guns and other valuables from theft and fire (provided your safe is fireproof—some lower-priced models aren't). These days every new firearm is supplied with a free gunlock. Use it—although safes are still the very best protection.

10. Don't mix alcohol and gunpowder. Never drink alcoholic beverages before or during a hunting or shooting session.

USE COMMON SENSE

That muzzle should never be allowed to point in an unsafe direction. That may sound like an impossible rule to follow, but it really isn't. If you can't point the gun downrange, keep it pointing safely skyward. (But remember, that bullet will come down somewhere. Sometimes "up" isn't a safe direction.) If you can't, for some reason, keep the muzzle up, point it at the ground. Never allow the muzzle to wander in the direction of another person. If your gun never points at anyone, you'll never accidentally shoot a man, woman, or child.

This rule applies whether or not you think the handgun is loaded. That little detail isn't really important. The first safety commandment tells you to treat *every* gun as if it were loaded—even if you're absolutely certain it's not.

The third commandment listed is really a corollary of the first two: Never point a gun at anything you don't intend to shoot. Unfortunately, there are always a few people stupid enough to point a gun in jest at a domestic animal or at another person. "I didn't really mean to shoot" or "I didn't know the gun was loaded" are cries sometimes heard. No handgun hunter should behave so stupidly.

RENDERING HANDGUNS INOPERABLE

The only time it's safe to relax the above cardinal rules is when the handgun has been partially dismantled, and can't possibly be made to fire. When not in use, double-action revolvers can be made inoperable if you crane the cylinder all the way to the side and hold the gun by the backstrap with your finger(s) occupying the space vacated by the cylinder.

Single-action revolvers can be rendered safely inoperable by removing the cylinder entirely from the gun. Remove the center pin holding the cylinder in place, open the loading gate in the right recoil shield, and move the cylinder to the right until it's clear of the frame. Then carry the gun by the top strap in the manner described above.

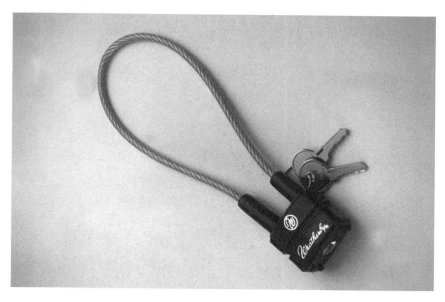

All new guns now come equipped with individual locks.

Auto pistols can be made totally harmless by removing the slide from the frame. However, it's more convenient to remove the magazine, and then lock the slide in the fully open position.

The safe-carry condition for single-shot pistols is with the action broken open to expose the empty chamber. Open the bolt on bolt-action handguns like the Savage Striker.

USE A SAFE BACKSTOP AND CLEARLY IDENTIFY YOUR TARGET

Whenever you shoot a firearm, you should do it only in an area where no person or domestic animal will be struck by flying bullets. Even a .22 rimfire bullet is still dangerous a mile or more from the muzzle.

The safest way to sight in or practice with your hunting handgun is to shoot into a high earthen bank or backstop. The backstop should be large enough to stop bullets that may miss the intended target by several yards. A large hillside or gravel pit makes a good practice site. When hunting, make sure of your target. Never shoot at sound or movement in the brush. Unless you can see the animal clearly and are sure of its identification, don't fire!

KEEP GUNS UNLOADED WHEN NOT IN USE

As soon as you're through at the shooting range, unload those guns! The same holds true whenever you leave the hunting field. Guns should be loaded only when you're preparing to shoot, and unloaded immediately afterward. Hunters shouldn't load their guns until they're in the field and ready to hunt. And unloaded or loaded, make sure the barrel never points at your guide or another hunter.

Check your guns to make sure there's no ammunition in the magazine or chamber before you enter a car with them, and repeat this inspection before you take the guns into the house.

A locking handgun safe is the best way to prevent shooting accidents in the home.

Transport handguns in a lockable, portable case for extra security.

CHECK THE BORE FOR OBSTRUCTIONS

Before you load your gun prior to hunting, it's an excellent idea to check the bore to be sure it's free of dirt, snow, or other obstructions. Make sure the action is open first or that the cylinder is clear of the frame. An object in the bore can ruin the firearm and may cause injury when you fire. Even a tiny obstruction can cause dangerously high pressures.

If firing your handgun produces unusually low recoil or a very mild report, stop shooting immediately. Then unload the gun and check the bore to make sure the bullet didn't lodge there. A reload that failed to receive a full powder charge (it happens) can drive the bullet into the bore with just enough force to lodge it in the rifling. Firing another round through the bore is guaranteed to destroy the barrel and possibly the entire handgun—at real danger to the shooter.

AVOID RICOCHETS

Shooting at water, rocks, or any hard surface can cause ricochets. These are dangerous because they're unpredictable—a ricochet can fly off at an angle to the right or left, and in some rare instances can even reverse field and head back toward the shooter.

Heavy bottle glass can also produce ricochets, particularly when hit by .22 rimfire bullets. Sharp shards of glass are unsightly and dangerous to pick up and remove. If they're left where they lie, they may injure the next person or animal that comes along. Leaving glass or other hazardous litter is also likely to result in "no trespassing" signs being posted, depriving you of a shooting site.

EYE AND EAR PROTECTION

Handgunners should wear shooter's earmuffs or earplugs designed for the sport whenever they fire guns. Even a .22 rimfire

It's important to wear effective eye and ear protection when shooting handguns.

revolver generates enough noise to permanently damage hearing. Repeated exposure to either centerfire or rimfire muzzle blast can eventually deafen you.

For practicing on the range, muff-type protectors are more effective than most commercial earplugs, although either can help prevent serious hearing damage. For plinking or target shooting, ear protection is a must. It will not only preserve your precious hearing, it will also boost your scores. Wearing ear protectors is the surest way to eliminate flinching, making shooting practice more enjoyable.

Handgunning hunters often don't bother with this kind of protection afield. When you're hunting, earmuffs can become hot, sweaty, and uncomfortable—although in very cold weather they provide welcome warmth. The best shooting muffs electronically enhance hearing (a boon to hunters), while providing protection against loud muzzle blast.

Custom and over-the-counter earplugs offering these same advantages are available, as well. Custom-fit earplugs will cost you a few hundred bucks, but that's cheap insurance. If your

Hoppe's folding sound muffler offers 28-decibel protection.

The innovative Walker's Game Ear fits inside the ear. It magnifies normal sound and protects the ear from high-decibel gunfire.

handgun barrel is ported or equipped with a muzzle brake, I'd highly advise wearing some form of hearing protection. If you don't want to bother with muffs or electronic devices, carry a handful of disposable plugs in your pocket. There's usually plenty of time to insert them once you spot game. Big magnum handguns can be—quite literally—deafening.

Eyes also deserve protection. Any glasses with hardened glass or plastic lenses will do, or you can purchase glasses designed specifically for shooting. If you're an aging handgunner (like me) you probably wear prescription glasses. Just be sure they have hardened lenses.

Punctured primers or failed cases are rare, but when they happen, hot gases containing powder and lead particles can spew back into the shooter's face. Some revolvers are notorious for spitting lead from the gap between barrel and cylinder, while autoloaders throw hot empty cases. When you shoot a handgun, eye protection is something you can't afford to do without.

FINAL THOUGHTS

Safe gun handling precludes practicing fast draws with a loaded pistol or revolver. "Fast draw" was once a popular sport among some handgunners, and there are still those who practice it. But fast draw has no place in the hunting field (unless you surprise an angry grizzly at close range). Handguns should always be treated with the respect they deserve.

Safety should always be uppermost in your mind whenever you hold or shoot a handgun. Mistakes made with a gun in your hand tend to be serious and permanent.

Properly used handguns are as safe as any recreational tool. But handled carelessly—even for a moment—they can turn deadly. For any hunter, firearm safety should be practiced until it becomes second nature. It's one habit you'll never want to break.

Chapter 16

CARE AND CLEANING

Today's handguns are tough and durable. Given the proper care, they can be counted on to function reliably and last a lifetime. Neglected, these same guns will become progressively less dependable—and hunters need perfect dependability. Abused handguns can deteriorate badly in a few short years.

If you ever plan to trade in or sell your handgun (something few dedicated hunters do), proper maintenance can help that firearm retain its value. While this is a worthwhile consideration, the most pressing reason to keep your handgun cleaned and properly lubricated is to keep it working safely and reliably. Moving parts should be kept free of dirt, debris, and powder deposits.

When lubricating those parts, do it very, very lightly. Leave just enough oil on bearing surfaces to prevent excessive friction and wear. Drowning a handgun's action in oil does more harm than good. It can gum things up more quickly than simple neglect.

The bore should be kept clean, with no metal fouling allowed to remain in the lands and grooves. Powder fouling also must be removed. When the gun isn't in use, be sure a light film of oil protects the bore.

Outer surfaces should be wiped with a silicone-impregnated or oiled cloth before the gun is put away after a shooting or hunting session. This keeps rust-causing fingerprints and moisture at bay. Checkered or stippled stocks should be kept free of grease and dirt. An old toothbrush helps with this chore, although any brush with nylon bristles will do.

CLEANING KITS

Keeping a handgun clean and in top working order is easy and requires only a few basic tools. You need a cleaning rod with a threaded tip to accept a bronze or nylon brush and a slotted or jagged tip to hold cloth patches in place. The cleaning rod must be long enough to pass completely through your handgun's barrel, regardless of length. The bronze brush you use should be

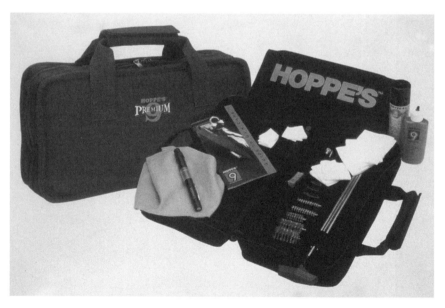

A good cleaning kit contains all tools and supplies needed to keep a handgun in good operating order.

sized to the bore, as should the tip that holds the cloth cleaning patches. You can use the same rod to clean everything from .22s to .50-caliber handguns, if necessary, but different accessory tips should be used for each caliber.

You also need a good powder solvent, lubricant, swabs, and a supply of properly sized cleaning patches (cotton works best). Don't forget one or more silicone-treated wiping cloths or oiled rags.

Outers, Marbles, Hoppe's and other companies market handgun-cleaning kits containing all of these items. A single such kit, with additional accessory tips to fit the different caliber guns you own, may provide all the cleaning tools you'll need for every handgun in your safe. Hoppe's handy BoreSnake kit includes a patented, bore-fitting pull cord with a built-in bronze brush and full-length flossing to clean dirty bores in a single pass. The kit also comes complete with bottles of Hoppe's famed No. 9 solvent and lubricating oil.

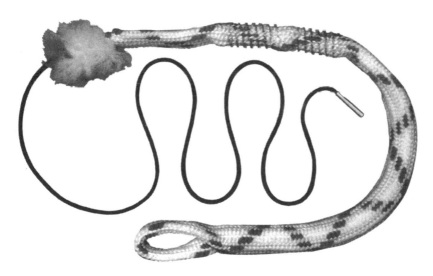

BoreSnake is a handy, all-in-one bore-cleaning tool.

Other useful cleaning items include an old toothbrush, a supply of cotton swabs, and a spray can of lubricant with a small plastic tube to allow you to place just the right amount of lubrication on hard-to-reach parts.

For removing stubborn lead deposits from a centerfire handgun bore, a device called the Lewis Lead Remover can be extremely helpful. It's basically a cleaning rod designed to force copper wire screens through a handgun's bore. The Lewis Lead Remover is particularly helpful if you own a gun with a bore that leads heavily and can't resist firing lead bullets through it at moderately high velocities.

HANDGUN DISASSEMBLY

All handguns must be periodically disassembled to allow thorough cleaning. You need the proper tools to do this job right. Quality square-bladed screwdrivers sized to fit each screw you'll be removing will prevent burred heads. A too-large or too-small blade will gouge and mar your guns. Rounded blades can be even more damaging, as they slip from the slot under pressure.

Detailed disassembly instructions should accompany each new handgun you buy. If your owner's manual is lost, write the manufacturer for a replacement. Never attempt to dismantle a revolver or auto pistol without knowing what you're doing. Check those instructions.

Auto pistols can usually be broken into main component groups without tools, and they should be partially dismantled before each cleaning. In disassembly, the magazine is always removed first. Then the slide is typically pulled all the way rearward as a takedown catch is released. (The location and operation of this takedown catch varies with make and model.) The slide is then tipped up at the rear and moved forward and off the frame. At this point the barrel can be removed from the slide assembly, and cleaning can begin.

Auto-pistol and single-shot handgun barrels should be cleaned from breech to muzzle—never the reverse. Cleaning from the muzzle end can damage rifling and affect accuracy. Most revolver barrels can be cleaned only from the muzzle, so care must be taken to keep the cleaning rod from scraping against the rifling. Dan Wesson revolvers are an exception. Dan Wesson barrels can be easily unscrewed and should always be cleaned from the breech.

HOW TO CLEAN, LUBRICATE, AND CARE FOR YOUR HANDGUN

The first step in cleaning the bore is to attach the bronze brush to your cleaning rod. Dip the brush in solvent—never use it dry—and scrub the bore vigorously. Remember to work from the rear of the barrel whenever possible. Use full strokes that push the brush completely through the bore; don't reverse direction until after the brush emerges at the other end.

Next, replace the bronze brush with the slotted or jagged tip, and fasten a cloth patch of the proper size. Wipe the bore with patches until they come out nearly clean. A light green cast remaining on the patch indicates traces of jacket copper in the bore and can be ignored. A heavy green-blue tint means you still have a lot of work to do.

Run the solvent-soaked brush through the bore several times again, followed by dry cloth patches. If deposits prove unusually stubborn, use a mild abrasive paste like J-B Compound on a tightly fitting cloth patch. Don't make a habit of it, though, as it can damage rifling if used improperly.

REMOVING LEADING AND METAL FOULING

The Lewis Lead Remover mentioned earlier is perfect for ridding your bore of stubborn lead deposits, usually caused by firing unjacketed, cast-lead bullets. The Lewis tool comes with instructions; follow them. If copper fouling is the problem, try using a solvent like Barnes CR-10, which is specifically designed to remove it.

After cleaning and drying the bore, inspect it against a light source for possible traces of fouling that may remain in the grooves. Such residues tend to accumulate along the edges of the grooves, in the comers. If fouling remains, repeat the cleaning process described above. When the barrel is finally clean, pass a lightly oiled patch through the bore.

When cleaning a revolver, follow the same general procedure with each chamber in the cylinder. Scrub lightly with a solvent-soaked brush, follow with dry patches, and finish up with a lightly oiled patch.

For general cleaning after shooting, a revolver or single-shot pistol needn't be taken apart. Simply clean and oil the bore and chamber(s). If a drop of oil is needed to lubricate the hinge pin or some other bearing sur-

A needle applicator allows precise placement of lubricant.

face, fine—but don't overdo it. A needle oiler is handy to ensure against over-oiling. Be sure to promptly wipe off any excess lubricant. Finally, wipe the metal surfaces with a lightly oiled or silicone-treated cloth to remove fingerprints, as these will eventually cause rust if left on a gun's surface.

When cleaning a taken-down auto pistol, use a nylon bristle brush or old toothbrush to remove dirt and powder deposits from the frame and the inside of the slide. Scrub the breech and make sure the extractor hook is clean. Then wipe with an oily cloth. Auto pistols can be fussy about too much gunk in their innards, so wise shooters will keep these handguns as clean as possible.

When more extensive cleaning becomes necessary—and this should be done periodically anyway—revolvers can be taken apart to bare their insides. The grips come off first. Some revolvers have removable sideplates held in place by screws. Once the screws are undone (remember to use a good screwdriver that fits), tapping the frame with a leather mallet or the rubberized handle of a screwdriver will loosen the sideplate, which can then be lifted free of the gun.

Other models feature solid frames and working parts that can be removed through the bottom of the frame once anchoring screws or pins are removed. Refer to the owner's manual accompanying your revolver before attempting disassembly.

Once the inner workings are bared, examine them carefully for possible corrosion and to see if they're clean and adequately lubricated. Unless you know what you're doing and are confident in your abilities to reassemble them properly, it's best to leave all those small, moving parts pretty much intact. If they appear dirty or gunked up, spray in some solvent and use a toothbrush, cotton swab, toothpick, or anything else that's handy and small enough to get the dirt free. Dry with a soft cloth or hairdryer, and then lightly oil surfaces that come in contact with each other.

Scrub under the top strap and across the barrel root to remove powder and lead residue. With double-action revolvers, remove the cylinder and make sure no dirt lurks under the ejector star. Keep both cylinder faces free of deposits and debris.

This kind of routine cleaning should keep your handgun in top shape. If your gun becomes soaked with water, it must be thoroughly dried inside and out, and re-lubricated to keep it from rusting. This must be done as soon as possible to halt corrosion in its earliest stages.

The easiest way to dry a water-soaked gun is to remove the wooden grips and place it in a two-hundred-degree oven for an hour or so. Don't subject it to high temperatures, which could be harmful. After the gun is dry, disassemble and lubricate lightly inside and out. Pressurized cans that deliver a very fine spray of lubricant work best.

STORING HANDGUNS

Don't leave your handgun in a fleece-lined case too long. Fleece can retain rust-promoting moisture. And never store guns in leather holsters. Prolonged contact with holster leather can also promote rusting. Whatever individual storage case you use, be sure everything is locked securely away in your gun safe.

If you live in a particularly humid climate, or if regular cleaning simply doesn't appeal to you, consider purchasing a stainless-steel firearm. Stainless-steel handguns are a bit more expensive than similar blued-steel models, but they're almost (but not completely) impervious to rust. A certain amount of lu-

When not in use, keep handguns locked safely away out of reach of children.

brication is needed to keep parts functioning properly, and the bore and action should still be cleaned after use. But stainless handguns can be neglected far longer than blued-steel guns with no ill effect.

Stainless-steel handguns are ideal for hunting, simply because they better withstand the effects of weather. If they're scratched or marred, a few passes of abrasive cloth will repair the damage.

GLOSSARY OF HANDGUNNING TERMS

Accuracy: The ability of a handgun (or shooter) to hit the mark or target aimed at with a bullet. An accurate handgun should be capable of placing successive shots very close together on the target.

ACP: Shorthand designation for Automatic Colt Pistol cartridges. Such cartridges aren't limited to use in Colt pistols, but will function in any handgun chambered for the round.

Action: The operating mechanism of a handgun.

Air gun or air pistol: A handgun that uses compressed air or CO_2 gas to propel a BB or skirted lead pellet.

Ammunition: The cartridges fired in a handgun. Each loaded cartridge consists of a metal case containing a primer, propellant powder, and a bullet. Air-gun ammunition consists of the BB or lead-pellet projectile.

Autoloader: A handgun that automatically feeds a fresh round into the firing chamber after the preceding round has been fired. Also called an automatic or semi-automatic.

Automatic: This term is used to describe semi-automatic handguns, although the only true automatic firearms are machine guns that continue to fire as long as the trigger is depressed. See *Autoloader*.

Backstop: Something used to stop the flight of bullets fired at a target.

Backstrap: The metal part of a handgun frame forming the rear of the grip.

Ball: A lead ball used in blackpowder handguns.

Ball ammunition: Full-jacketed pistol ammunition.

Ballistics: The study of bullets in flight.

Barrel: The hollow steel tube through which bullets are fired.

Battery: Describes the condition of a handgun that has the action closed and ready to fire.

BB: A spherical copper-plated shot used in air pistols.

Big Bore: An appellation used for handguns and handgun cartridges of greater than .38 caliber.

Blackpowder: An early propellant powder used in firearms. Although obsolete, it is still used in modern replicas and other handguns designed specifically for this powder.

Blank: A cartridge loaded without a bullet. It is used to produce noise only, although powder burns can result if a blank-firing handgun is pointed at someone at close range.

Blowback: An auto-pistol action that is forced open by the rearward pressure on the fired cartridge case.

Bluing (or blueing): A dark blue-black finish applied to steel handgun parts as a rust preventative.

Bore: The interior of a barrel.

Brass: A term sometimes used to describe an empty cartridge case.

Break-top: A revolver or single-shot handgun that opens at the breech by unlocking the action and tipping the hinged barrel downward.

Breech: The chamber end of a barrel and/or that part of the gun's action immediately behind the firing chamber.

Bull barrel: A heavy, thick barrel typically used on target handguns.

Bullet: The projectile fired from a handgun. The term is usually reserved for cartridge-loaded projectiles. Air guns fire BBs or pellets, while blackpowder handguns fire lead balls.

Bullet energy: The force with which a bullet strikes its target, expressed in foot-pounds.

Bullet mold: A mold used by handloaders in casting bullets from hot lead.

Bullet trap: A container used to stop fired bullets.

Bull's-eye: The round center part of a target that produces the highest score when hit. Also the trade name for a popular handgun powder used in reloading.

Butt: The bottom end of a handgun's grip.

Caliber: The diameter of a handgun's bore, measured in hundredths of an inch or in millimeters. May also be used to designate bullet diameter.

Cannon lock: A means of ignition used on early firearms. The powder charge was ignited by passing a flame through a hole bored into the barrel directly over the firing chamber.

Cap: Percussion cap used to detonate the main powder charge in blackpowder cap-and-ball handguns.

Cap and ball: Describes a pistol or revolver loaded with a lead ball and blackpowder, with a percussion cap used to ignite the powder charge.

Caplock: A firing mechanism in which a percussion cap is crushed by a spring-loaded hammer to provide ignition of the main blackpowder charge.

Cartridge: Handgun ammunition containing a primer, powder, and a bullet in the same metallic case.

Case: The metallic container that holds the primer, powder, and bullet.

Case head separation: A cartridge-case failure in which the case head or base separates from the cartridge body.

Case mouth: The open end of a cartridge case.

Centerfire: A handgun or cartridge that uses a removable primer located in the base of the cartridge to ignite the powder charge.

Chamber: That portion of a pistol barrel or revolver cylinder in which cartridges are inserted for firing.

Clip: Often refers to the detachable box magazine used in auto pistols. More correctly, a metal device holding several cartridges, which allows them to be inserted through the top of the breech in a single movement.

Crane: The steel yoke that holds the cylinder of a double-action revolver. The crane is hinged at the bottom to allow the cylinder to swing clear of the frame for loading or unloading.

Creep: Movement of the trigger after pressure is applied and before the hammer begins to fall.

Crimp: Pressure applied to the mouth of the cartridge case to hold the bullet in place.

Cylinder: A cylindrical piece of steel with firing chambers enclosed within its circumference, used in revolvers.

Cylinder gap: The space that exists between the rear of the barrel and the forward edge of a revolver's cylinder. If this gap is excessive, hot gas and bits of metal may be exhausted through it when the revolver is fired.

Cylinder latch: The catch that locks the cylinder crane to the frame.

Derringer: A small pocket handgun, usually with one or two single-shot barrels.

Double action: A term used to describe handguns that can be fired simply by pulling the trigger without first cocking the gun manually.

Ear protectors: Devices worn in or over a shooter's ears to protect against hearing loss caused by gunfire.

Ejection: The act of forcefully removing a spent cartridge case or an unfired cartridge from the action of a firearm.

Ejector: A mechanical device that causes ejection.

Ejector rod: In a revolver, the rod that extends forward from the cylinder below or along the barrel. Pushing rearward on this rod causes the ejector to function—once the loading gate (single action) is open or the cylinder (double action) has been swung clear of the frame.

Elevation: The vertical movement of an adjustable sight. Changing the elevation of a sight raises or lowers the bullet strike on target.

Expanding bullet: A bullet with a hollow point or an exposed tip of soft lead, designed to expand on impact.

Extraction: The removal, or partial removal, of a spent cartridge case or unfired round from a gun's chamber.

Extractor: A device that pushes or pulls at the base of a cartridge case to cause extraction.

Extractor groove: The recessed groove just forward of the cartridge case base in rimless auto-pistol cartridges. This groove accommodates the extractor.

Eye relief: The distance required between the shooter's eye and the eyepiece lens of a scope sight to allow a full field of view. Scopes designed for handgun use typically have an eye relief of twelve inches or more.

Fanning: A technique for firing a single-action revolver rapidly by holding the trigger back, then using the heel of the free hand to rapidly and repeatedly strike the back of the hammer. This practice is dangerous and can damage the gun.

Fast draw: Rapidly drawing a handgun from a holster. This also describes a competition in which shooters draw and fire blanks while being timed by a stopwatch.

Feed guide: A ramp or guide projecting rearward a short way from a pistol's firing chamber. The guide is intended to guide the cartridge into the chamber.

Feeding: The act of introducing a loaded cartridge into a gun's firing chamber, either manually or by mechanical means.

Feet per second (fps): The number of feet a bullet travels in a single second.

Finish: The treatment applied to the metal or wood parts of a handgun to preserve or cosmetically enhance them.

Firearm: A mechanism used to propel a bullet or other projectile at high speed by the pressure of expanding gases from a burning powder charge. Also, any type of gun.

Firing line: The position from which gunners shoot.

Firing pin: A small steel cylinder driven by a hammer or striker into the primer of a cartridge to initiate the combustion process.

Flyer: A lone bullet strike well outside the group of holes made by the other bullets fired.

Frame: The main part of a revolver containing the working mechanism and holding the barrel rigidly in place. Or in an auto pistol, that major portion of the gun containing all the working parts not part of the slide assembly.

Free pistol: A highly specialized target handgun used primarily in European competition.

Front sight: The vertical blade sight found near the muzzle.

Gas check: A shallow copper cup attached to the base of a lead bullet to protect the lead from hot gases.

Grip: That part of a handgun designed to be enclosed in the shooter's hand.

Grip adapter: A small filler attached behind the trigger guard of a handgun to better position the hand.

Grip safety: A mechanical safety device incorporated into the backstrap of some auto pistols. The safety is automatically disengaged when the gun is gripped in firing position.

Grooves: The shallow rifling cuts made in the bore of a handgun or rifle.

Gun: See *Firearm*.

Gun control: A term referring to any legislative act or proposal designed to control the sale, ownership, and/or use of guns.

Gunpowder: The propellant material burned in a firing chamber to force a projectile out the bore.

Hair trigger: A trigger that requires very little pressure to begin the firing sequence.

Half cock: A hammer position somewhere between fully cocked and fully forward. Used primarily in reloading or unloading some single-action revolvers.

Hammer: A spring-powered device that pivots forward to strike the firing pin after the trigger is pulled.

Hammer block: A device that blocks the hammer, preventing contact with the firing pin.

Hammerless: A pistol that uses an internal striker mechanism in place of a hammer to activate the firing pin.

Hammer spur: The serrated projection at the top of a hammer used to provide leverage for the shooter's thumb in cocking the hammer.

Hand: The mechanical arm that rotates the cylinder of a revolver as the gun is cocked.

Handgun: A relatively compact firearm designed to be fired by one hand, although two hands are often used.

Handloading: Replacing the expended primer, powder, and bullet in a fired cartridge case so that the cartridge can again be fired.

Hangfire: A delay between the time the hammer falls and the time the gun actually fires. May be caused by faulty ammunition.

Headspace: The distance between the breech face and that part of the chamber that supports the cartridge against the firing-pin blow.

Hollowpoint: A bullet with a hollow cavity in its nose, designed to expand when it strikes game.

Holosight: Bushnell trademark describing a type of red-dot sight that uses a holographic aiming reticle.

Holster: A sheath or case worn strapped to the body, in which a handgun is carried.

Inertia firing pin: A frame-mounted firing pin that is held away from the cartridge primer by spring pressure until struck by the hammer or striker.

Iron sights: Any metallic sights in which glass lenses are not used.

Jacket: The metallic sheath covering a bullet's lead core.

Jag: A cylindrical, grooved cleaning-rod tip used to hold cloth patches.

Jam: Any condition that prevents the mechanical operation of a firearm.

JHP: Jacketed hollowpoint bullet designed to expand on impact.

JSP: Jacketed softpoint bullet.

Keyholing: A hole made in a target by a bullet yawing, or tumbling, in flight.

Lands: The raised surfaces between grooves in a rifled bore.

Leading: Deposits of lead left in a rifled bore after firing.

Loading gate: A hinged gate, usually on the right recoil shield of a single-action revolver, which provides access to each firing chamber as the cylinder is manually rotated.

Loading press: A tool used for reloading centerfire cartridges.

Lock time: The elapsed time between trigger pull and cartridge ignition.

Lockwork: The operating mechanism of a handgun.

Long Rifle: A term used to designate the longest version of popular .22 rimfire ammunition.

Magazine: A container for the ammunition supply carried in an auto pistol.

Magazine safety: A device that prevents an auto pistol from firing if the magazine is removed.

Magnum: A term used to designate an extremely powerful gun or cartridge.

Mainspring: The spring that powers the hammer or striker.

Match: Organized shooting competition.

Match ammunition: Ammunition designed specifically for target use.

Matchlock: A fifteenth-century method of firearm ignition that used a slow-burning fuse fitted in a mechanical arm to ignite the powder charge.

Misfire: The failure of a cartridge to fire after the primer has been struck by the firing pin.

Muzzle: The foremost end of a gun barrel.

Muzzle brake: Some alteration made to the muzzle of a gun to reduce recoil or muzzle jump.

Muzzle energy: The striking force of a projectile as it exits the muzzle.

Muzzleloader: A type of blackpowder gun that must be loaded from the muzzle, not the breech.

Muzzle velocity: The speed (in feet per second) of a bullet as it leaves the muzzle.

National Rifle Association (NRA): An organization dedicated to shooting sports, based in Washington, D.C.

Nipple: The projecting, hollow seat on which a percussion cap is placed.

Overtravel: Continuing movement of the trigger after the hammer or striker has been released.

Patch: A cloth patch forced through the bore on a cleaning rod.

Patridge sight: An adjustable target sight that features a squared-off front sight blade with a flat-topped rear sight.

Pellet: A pointed, cylindrical lead projectile with a flared skirt, fired from air guns.

Percussion cap: A fulminate-filled, cup-shaped metal container used to ignite blackpowder.

Percussion gun: Any gun that uses a percussion cap to initiate firing.

Percussion lock: The lockwork in a percussion firearm.

Pistol: Often used as a generic term for all handguns, it is more accurately used to describe single-shot bolt-action and autoloading handguns.

Plinking: Informal shooting practice at any of a variety of targets.

Powder charge: The amount of gunpowder used in a cartridge.

Primer: A cup-shaped device containing an explosive mixture that detonates when the primer is partially crushed by the firing pin. This detonation in turn ignites the main propellant charge in the cartridge. The primer is located in the base of the cartridge.

Primer pocket: The pocket in the base of the cartridge case that's designed to contain the primer.

Projectile: The bullet, or anything fired from a gun.

Psi: Abbreviation of "pounds per square inch."

Propellant: The powder charge burned in a cartridge to produce the expanding gases needed to force the projectile down and out the bore.

Range: The distance from shooter to target. Also, an area used for shooting.

Recoil: The rear-moving forces caused by firing a projectile in the opposite direction.

Recoil shield: The metal flange projecting from either side of a revolver's frame immediately behind the cylinder. This shield prevents loaded cartridges from backing out of their chambers under recoil.

Red-dot sight: An optical sight featuring a battery-powered aiming dot, usually used on handguns.

Reloading: See *Handloading.*

Resizing: Squeezing an expanding cartridge case back to its original diameter by passing it through a reloading die designed for this purpose.

Revolver: A handgun that holds cartridges in individual firing chambers contained in a revolving steel cylinder.

Rib: A flat strip of raised metal affixed to the top of a barrel.

Ricochet: The unpredictable movement of a bullet after it strikes a hard, unyielding surface.

Rifling: The lands and grooves cut into a gun bore in a spiral pattern. They impart stabilizing spin to the bullet as it passes through the bore.

Rim: The projecting edge at the base of a cartridge.

Rimfire: A cartridge with the priming compound contained in the rim of the case.

Round: A single cartridge.

Safety: A mechanical device that prevents accidental firing of a gun.

Sear: The device that holds the hammer or striker in the cocked position until the trigger is pulled.

Semi-automatic: A pistol that automatically reloads and cocks itself after every firing. An auto pistol.

Shell holder: A device that grips the rim of a cartridge case to hold the case in the loading press.

Shooting glasses: Eyeglasses with hardened lenses, designed specifically for shooting.

Short: The short configuration of the popular .22 rimfire cartridge.

Shot cartridge: A handgun cartridge loaded with multiple tiny pellets in place of a single bullet or projectile.

Shoulder holster: A holster worn over the shoulder that holds the gun high on the shooter's chest or under the armpit.

Sidearm: A handgun or other small, easily carried firearm.

Sight: Any device used to aim a firearm.

Sighting in: Adjusting a firearm's sights so that the bullet strikes where the sights are pointed.

Sight radius: The distance between front and rear sights.

Silencer: A device used to muffle the report of a firearm. Silencers are illegal in most countries unless accompanied by a special license.

Single action: A term describing handguns that must be manually cocked before being fired.

Six o'clock hold: A method of sighting in where the front sight blade is positioned immediately under the bull's-eye.

Slide: The reciprocating housing that covers the barrel and striker mechanism in an auto pistol.

Smallbore: A term used for .22-caliber guns and ammunition.

Striker: A spring-activated device released by pulling the trigger. It then moves forward to strike the rear of the firing pin.

Target: Any object at which a firearm is fired. Often refers to printed-paper targets.

Top strap: The solid top portion of a revolver's frame.

Trajectory: The curved path of a bullet in flight.

Trigger: The exposed part of the firing mechanism pressed by the shooter's finger to initiate the firing process.

Trigger guard: The metal or plastic loop encircling the trigger.

Trigger stop: A mechanical projection that limits rearward travel of the trigger.

Velocity: The speed of a bullet in flight, usually expressed in feet per second (fps).

Ventilated rib: A sighting rib elevated above the barrel by a series of rests or posts.

Wadcutter: A flat-nosed bullet designed to cut sharp, clearly defined holes in a paper target.

Wax bullet: A bullet made of wax, for indoor practice.

Wheel lock: An early firearm lock that produced ignition by spinning a serrated wheel against a piece of flint or pyrite to generate sparks.

Wildcat: A nonstandard cartridge not commercially available.

Windage: Horizontal sight adjustment to move the bullet's point of impact to the left or right.

WMRF: Winchester Magnum Rimfire, a .22-caliber cartridge of greater power than the popular .22 Long Rifle load. Not interchangeable with the .22 Long Rifle, although some revolvers are made with two cylinders to allow the use of both kinds of ammunition in the same handgun.

Yoke: The revolver crane.

Zero: To adjust the sights so the bullet impacts point of aim.

INDEX